for Lu, Jason and Caroline

BACKPACKING

BASICS

Enjoying the mountains with friends and family

Thomas Winnett
with Melanie Findling

FIRST EDITION 1972 (entitled *Backpacking for Fun*)
Second printing April 1976
SECOND EDITION April 1979
Second printing July 1981
Third printing February 1983
Fourth printing August 1985
THIRD EDITION March 1988
FOURTH EDITION March 1994
Second printing June 1995

Front cover photo © 1994 by Ed Cooper
Drawings by Don Denison, Lucille Winnett,
            Jeffrey P. Schaffer and Larry Van Dyke
Design by Thomas Winnett and Kathy Morey
Cover design by Larry Van Dyke

Library of Congress Card Catalog Number 93-50548
International Standard Book Number 0-89997-172-5

Printed in the United States of America

Published by Wilderness Press
              2440 Bancroft Way
              Berkeley, CA 94704
              (510)843-8080

Write for free catalog

Library of Congress Cataloging-in-Publication Data

Winnett, Thomas.
    Backpacking Basics / Thomas Winnett and Melanie Findling. — 4th ed.
        p.   cm.
    Includes bibliographical references (p.) and index.
    ISBN 0-89997-172-5
    1. Backpacking. I. Findling, Melanie. II. Title.
    GV199.6.W56 1994
    796.5'1—dc20
                                              93-50548
                                              CIP

Preface to the Fourth Edition

The first edition of this book, entitled *Backpacking for Fun,* came out when the sport of backpacking was at the peak of its growth phase. The great growth had a number of results, and they are the reasons new editions have been needed.

For one thing, the large number of campers in the backcountry made a new wilderness ethic imperative. It would no longer do to treat the backcountry as if it could supply burnable wood, pure water and untouched scenery infinitely. In some areas, the authorities now prohibit wood fires and require that you camp at least 100 feet from lake or stream. Even if they didn't, any sensible, sensitive backpacker would see that henceforth he must conserve wood and not pollute the water. Hence this edition has more about stoves and about sanitation than earlier editions.

The growth of the market for backpacking gear and clothing attracted many businessmen, and recent years have seen the application of much technology to the production of gear and clothing. Hence this edition has more about freeze-dried food, internal-frame packs, Gore-Tex and similar fabrics, polypropylene, fleece and vapor-barrier garments than earlier editions.

The increasing demand for places to backpack led to the growth of existing conservation groups and the formation of new ones. Groups like the Wilderness Society are engaged in a struggle to preserve America's wild places and, if possible, create new wilderness areas where roads and machines are not allowed. Hence this edition has an appendix that lists some organizations, in the hope that you will lend a hand.

Thomas Winnett

Table of Contents

Chapter 1. Getting Started 1
Chapter 2. Equipment 5
Chapter 3. Clothing 29
Chapter 4. Food and Cooking 39
Chapter 5. Day Hikes—A Prelude 53
Chapter 6. Planning Trips 55
Chapter 7. Trailhead Tips 65
Chapter 8. Walking 67
Chapter 9. Camping Techniques 73
Chapter 10. Safety and Well-being 91
Chapter 11. Map and Compass 103
Chapter 12. Equipment Care 107
Chapter 13. Taking Children 111
Chapter 14. Recommended Reading 121
Appendix I. Mail-Order Companies with Backpacking
     Equipment, and Mail-Order Lightweight Food Stores ... 125
Appendix II. Checklist for Packing 127
Appendix III. Conservation Organizations 129
Author's Pack 131
Index 134

1

• • • • • • • • • • • • • • • • • •

Getting Started

The other day I asked a friend why he had never gone back-packing. "I'd like to," he said, "but I wouldn't know what to do."

This book will tell you how to make the first trip. Once you have done that, you will probably do a lot more backpacking on your own.

Backpacking is a way to go anywhere, any time. With your "house" on your back, you can stop when and where you like. You can spend your entire life backpacking—if money is no problem—pausing only to buy more food and, once in a while, new boots. Backpacking is the cheapest way to travel in the wilderness, and almost the only way. Some people will go in on horses, but in recent years their numbers have not grown, while the number of backpackers has grown considerably.

Why? People have more leisure time, of course. New highways have made wilderness areas much nearer in driving time. Lightweight, durable backpacking equipment is widely available, and dehydrated and freeze-dried foods have been developed. But the main reason is that city life has begun to drive us crazy. People need to spend some time where it is utterly uncrowded and quiet, where they can renew their perspective on life. To get to such a place, you have to walk.

Another reason for the growing popularity of backpacking is that it is the cheapest, least polluting, and least energy-using form of recreation. In an age when oil supplies may be cut off at any time or may become terribly expensive, backpacking becomes especially attractive.

Exactly what do you need in order to go backpacking? All you really need is the desire to do it. If you have that, nothing else is essential. Some books say you need two feet, but I have seen amputees in the wilderness with their children. Some books say you need a warm sleeping bag, but John Muir, the backpacker's saint, never carried one. He didn't even carry a blanket. Some books say you need a sturdy, lightweight pack, but I have seen people miles from their automobile carrying everything they needed in two suitcases.

Despite my great affection for people like that, I am in favor of sufficient, comfortable equipment. In the next chapters I will recommend the equipment and the clothing. But what I'm saying here is, if you *want* to get away from city life into some unspoiled country for a few days, you *can*.

Chances are you have already gone camping. Then you know how beautiful and how quiet the outdoors can be. Unfortunately, you also know how littered and ruined some campgrounds are, and how much noise fifty cars arriving in camp around 11 P.M. can make. When you were camping, you probably took a short walk away from the roads and the cars. You began to think about what it might be like to spend all night away from your car. Would I, you wondered, be able to make it? Could I build a fire, even in the rain? Could I fall asleep on the ground? What if a big animal came by in the night? And could I find my way back out?

It is only human to fear the unfamiliar, to worry about doing anything for the first time. Yet the most dangerous part of a backpacking trip is the drive to the trailhead! Wild animals give humans a very wide berth; you should be so lucky as to see a mountain lion. The only real dangers are getting lost, getting overchilled and having a bad fall, and you can avoid these if you use simple caution and common sense.

This book will tell you the how-to of backpacking: what equipment you need, and what techniques of wilderness camping you should learn. It will describe the most restful way to walk, and it will prepare you for possible emergencies. It will do this simply. The most important word for the backpacker—if not for everyone—is "simplify." Therefore, this book will leave out various detailed directions and instructions that some people might like to see included, but it won't leave out anything you really need to know.

2

Equipment

The first law of backpacking is, *you must carry everything.* Since your pack must not be too heavy or bulky, what you carry must be carefully and thoughtfully planned. Your equipment must be right and light. For your first trip, you might well spend twelve hours packing things, using a checklist that is complete down to "pants," as if you might walk out the door not wearing any. If you get pleasure out of careful preparation, you will also spend a lot of time preparing. And if you do that, you will be able to spend two weeks in the back country with plenty of food, clothing and shelter, and maybe with a few luxuries to reward you for your effort. Other people can't wait so long to get going, and they sometimes forget something, but it never seems to be anything they absolutely can't do without.

If you have been camping, you already own some equipment that is usable for backpacking. Maybe later you will want to replace some things with lighter or better versions. For now, save your money for the backpacking gear you will need right away.

The most expensive items of gear—as distinguished from clothing—are: boots, pack, sleeping bag and tent. The first three you need on every trip; the last you need on some.

Boots

Your feet have to carry both you and your pack, so be nice to them. They will be happy in a good pair of leather or leather-and-cloth boots. Tennis shoes and running shoes are not sturdy enough for wilderness trails, and at stream crossings and in wet meadows they immediately get soaked.

Good boots are not heavy boots. The U.S. Army Research Institute of Environmental Medicine found that it takes more than six times as much energy to carry a pound on your feet as on your back. In other words, saving a pound in the weight of your boots is just as good as removing six pounds from your pack.

Good hiking boots, ones that are sturdy enough for backpacking, can be expensive—over $100. The uppers should be leather or a combination of leather and fabric (like cordura, a very durable kind of nylon). They should cover your ankles, for stability. The more rugged the terrain you plan to hike in and the heavier your pack, the fewer seams, the thicker leather and the less fabric you'll want. Comfort is important, of course, so don't buy a boot stiffer or heavier than you will need. The soles should be of carbon-rubber, not leather (too slippery) or crepe or neoprene (not tough enough).

The fit of boots in any given size varies substantially from company to company. Try on a variety of boots from different manufacturers to determine which *last* (the form the boot is constructed on) feels best for you. If possible, try on boots toward the end of the day, when your feet will have swelled a bit from the day's activities.

Wear the socks you plan to wear on the trail. First check the boots' arch area to see that there is a solid shank to reinforce the curve of the arch. Then press down on the toe to make sure that it too is reinforced; a soft toe invites hurt feet. The back of the boot, around the heel, should also be reinforced to protect against impact and to keep your heel in place inside the boot. Put your foot in the boot, unlaced, and slide your toes forward until they touch the toe of the boot. There should just be room for your forefinger inside the boot behind your heel. Now lace the boots firmly and stand up. Wiggle your toes. They should not touch the end of the boot. The back of the boot should feel fairly snug around your heel. When you lift your heel, it may slide up a bit inside the boot, but once the boot is broken in, it should not. If the fit is right, the widest part of the boot will be about at the ball of your foot. (If you have very long toes, you will have to fit for length, rather than for position of the ball of your foot.)

The final store test is to stand on a sloping surface, facing downslope, to check that your foot does not slide forward and press your toes against the end of the boot.

Having bought your boots, *walk in them for a few days* to break them in before you begin your trip.

Thick wool socks provide cushioning and warmth, and soak up sweat well. A thinner pair of polypro, cotton or silk worn inside these is a great defense against blisters. (Chapter 10 discusses the blister problem.)

The Pack

Backpacks underwent a revolution right after World War II, with the invention of the contoured aluminum packframe. Properly packed, this rig puts most of the pack's weight on the hips and keeps the rest of the weight close to the body, almost over the body's center of gravity. (The same is true of packs with internal frames, which are discussed below under the heading "Internal-frame packs.") If your other gear is fairly heavy, you really need a good pack.

What frame you choose depends on—besides cost—your size. The fit of the frame is very important: an ill-fitting frame will be less comfortable with a 30-pound load than a well-fitting frame with a 40-pound load. When you put on an empty pack, the shoulder-strap attachments to the frame should be about one inch higher than where the straps cross your shoulders, and the band that goes across your lower back should be just below the point where your back starts to curve outward toward your rump. Obviously, this band must rest on the outward-sloping part of your back if it is to put most of the pack's weight on your pelvis rather than on your shoulders. (The position of the band is adjustable, within limits, on most frames, and some recent designs have a way to adjust *one* frame for any size adult.) When you add weight to the pack, the points I described will be about an inch lower.

External-frame pack

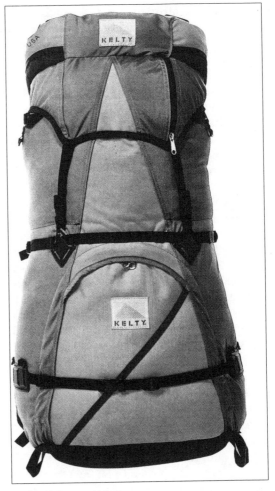

Internal-frame pack

The transfer of weight to the pelvis is performed by a hip belt—sometimes two separate straps, one attached to the bottom of each side of the frame, but more often a fully encircling belt attached to the frame in several places. This arrangement forms a tight circle that transfers most of the pack's weight onto the hip bones. Most hip belts are padded for comfort. Separate slip-on hip pads are available if you find that the hip belt cuts into your hips.

Some packframe designs have metal extending *forward* from the bottom of each side of the frame, and a wraparound belt attached to this metal at each side of your pelvis. This design allows the wraparound belt to pivot independently of the rest of the frame, and I find that more comfortable.

Whatever kind of belt you have, the way to tighten it is to first hunch up your shoulders as high as you can, or have someone lift your pack, and then tighten the belt as much as you can around the top of your hip bones without making your belly uncomfortable. The circle formed by the hip belt and the back band or by the wraparound belt should be horizontal—that is, parallel to the ground—and it should be just below the tops of your hipbones. When selecting a pack for fit, put some weight in the pack and make these tests with the belt. If the belt works loose when you walk, the buckle is faulty or you have threaded the belt through the buckle incorrectly.

Some metal packframes have a curved bar across the top, attached to the vertical sidebars or continuous with them. The bar aids in attaching things at the top of the pack. The bar also keeps the packbag away from your head. Depending on your body build and your posture, you may need such a bar. Without it, your packbag may push your head forward and thus strain your neck, to say nothing of knocking your hat off from time to time.

If you have the right-size pack and a properly fitting hip belt, almost no weight will be on your shoulders unless you choose to put some there by loosening the belt a little and tightening the shoulder straps a little. With nearly all the weight on your hips, your shoulder straps will merely keep the pack from falling backward.

Considering the cost of a packframe and bag, you might borrow or rent an outfit of the kind and size you think you prefer before buying.

Choose a packbag that will hold as much as you want to carry, and has enough pockets to suit you. I like as many pockets as I can get, because they allow me to put first aid here, fishing gear there, and lunch someplace else. Lots of pockets also help me find things in the dark. I also prefer horizontal to vertical pocket zippers, so that things don't fall out. To me, a separate compartment below the bag's main compartment, reached through a full-width zipper opening, is a must.

Some bags have sewn-in dividers in the main compartment. Although these help in organizing things, the resulting compartments are too small for some things I often carry, like a 4-quart cooking pot and my capacious 2-person tent in its stuff sack.

For the packbag materials, I recommend waterproof nylon—although in a heavy rain some water will work its way through the seams and under the flap anyway. To minimize water penetration, paint the seams with seam sealer and choose a bag with a long cover flap. A long flap is also desirable when you pack is brim-full and you must carry your sleeping bag or foam pad on top, under the flap. A waterproof pack cover will keep your pack contents dry under most adverse conditions. You can buy or make a form-fitted, coated-nylon rain cover, or use a large, heavy-duty garbage bag with holes cut for shoulder straps and hip belt. Such a cover is also handy for covering your pack at night if you don't want it in the tent.

There are numerous ways of tightening down the flap of the packbag, and numerous kinds of zippers. Some are easier to work than others, so check these features on the packbag you are thinking of buying.

Internal-Frame Packs

The development of the kind of pack described above was a major revolution in pack design. Another, more recent revolution was the development of large packs which have no exterior frame but which nevertheless can transfer most of the weight to your hips. This transfer requires attaching lengths of aluminum, stiff foam, or plastic to the packbag's fabric. Once the pack is stuffed properly, the entire unit becomes fairly rigid and can transfer weight to your hips through the hip belt.

Internal-frame packs are designed for mountaineering, backcountry skiing, and carrying loads over uneven terrain—activities in which there is more upper-body movement and more balance is required. The pack will flex as you lean over, reach for handholds, or swing your arms as you ski. In addition, it fits closer to your back and the load rides lower than with an external-frame pack, lowering your center of gravity for better balance. The profile of an internal-frame pack is narrower than that of an external-frame pack, and hence less likely to get caught on tree limbs along your path.

While internal-frame packs work quite well for backpacking, they have disadvantages compared with external-frame packs. For one thing, internal-frame packs were generally designed for smaller loads than external-frame packs, and they don't have the capacity for the loads required for trips of over about one week. They also have fewer compartments and pockets to help keep all your equipment organized, and fewer places outside the pack to attach gear. An internal-frame pack requires more care in packing to keep the weight properly distributed, and once the pack is full, it is more difficult to get at items that are buried deep in it. Internal-frame packs are also more expensive than external-frame packs.

Internal-frame packs can be more easily handled as luggage on plane flights, bus rides, etc. Some internal-frame packs even convert into suitcases called travel packs. After you zip a built-in fabric flap over the hip belt and the shoulder straps, the pack looks like a soft suitcase, and the damageable suspension system is protected. On most, the suspension system is compromised in favor of the suitcase design, yielding a pack that is suitable only for light loads carried for short periods. A travel pack—or any pack—suitable for backpacking needs to have a suspension system that will allow the weight of the load to be carried mostly on the hips, with the shoulder straps primarily keeping the pack from falling backward. The packbag needs to have compartments and/

or several compression straps to hold the load in place. (Compression straps are straps on the outside of the pack which tighten around the pack to hold the contents in place.) These features are typically found in the largest and most expensive models.

As for fit, the suspension systems on most internal-frame packs are adjustable. Help from someone experienced in fitting packs is important, to insure the proper adjustment. When the pack is loaded with gear or weights, the hip belt should squeeze the crest of your hips. The shoulder straps should rest evenly on your shoulders, with the stabilizer straps (attached from the shoulder straps to the top of the "frame") angling upward from your collarbone to the pack "frame." The sternum strap should cross the center of your chest. In some packs the aluminum stays can be bent to custom-fit the pack to the contours of your back. When choosing a pack, try a variety of brands and models to see which suspension system is most comfortable for you. And as you shop, keep in mind the pocket arrangement that will best fit your own needs. A feature some models of pack offer is a detachable hip or day pack, which replaces the need to carry an additional day pack if you plan to do much day hiking.

The Sleeping Bag

In the desert and in lowlands, a dacron sleeping bag can be fine, but for mountain backpacking a well-made sleeping bag filled with goose down or one of the newer synthetics is desirable—if not essential. It can be compressed into a small sack for carrying, and yet it fluffs up thick enough to provide warmth in freezing temperatures or even lower. Goose down gives more warmth per ounce than any other material. An ounce of good down will take up 600 cubic inches of space, but will compress to only about 15 cubic inches for carrying. A good goose-down sleeping bag that you can stuff into a football helmet will fluff up to give you two or three inches of blanket on top of your body.

The smallest bags are "mummy-shaped," widest at the shoulders and tapered at each end. Some people, however, need more width. Sleeping on my side in a slim mummy bag, I wake up

Top to bottom: mummy bag, modified mummy, rectangular bag.

every time I try to draw up my knees inside the bag and can't. So I use a modified mummy shape, which tapers only a little. It weighs about 25 percent more for the same amount of warmth, and it occupies about 25 percent more space in the pack. Mummy bags are more efficient at keeping you warm. The less sleeping bag your body has to heat up, the sooner you will be warm and the less likely the bag is to develop cold spots during the night.

If you shop thoughtfully for a sleeping bag, you will probably get pretty much what you pay for. You pay more for better-grade down or synthetic, and you pay more for a more intricate pattern of dividers inside the bag to keep the down or synthetic from shifting around. You also pay more for better stitching, and for better fabric. Finally, you pay more for more "loft"—the thickness of the whole bag, *top and bottom,* when it is shaken out flat. Ten inches of loft should be enough on top of Mount McKinley; don't buy that much if you are not going to sleep in such a cold place. If you are an average person, then four inches of loft will probably keep you warm at any temperature above freezing—*if* your sleeping bag and everything you are wearing is dry, *if* you are out of the wind, and *if* your head is inside the bag. The last is a good reason to buy a bag with a hood.

Since the four inches of loft is the thickness of the whole bag, about two inches will be above you. Beneath you, the bag will compress, and there will be far less than two inches of thickness. That's why you will need a mattress (see below).

Often, manufacturers describe the warmth of the bag in terms of a temperature *rating* rather than loft. These ratings are not standardized in the outdoor industry, so tend to be subjective. Temperature ratings do take into account variations in bag design such as having a hood and a collar that will increase warmth without adding loft. I know that a bag rated to 15 degrees above zero will not keep *me* warm at 15 degrees, and probably not at 25 degrees either, but I tend to sleep cold. It will, however, probably be adequate for late spring through fall trips when the temperature doesn't drop much below freezing, and I wear my long underwear and pile jacket inside. Someone who sleeps warm, however, may be quite comfortable in the colder temperatures without additional clothing layers. Because there's so much variation in how warm different people sleep, and variation in how warm any person will sleep under different conditions depending on how tired, hungry or thirsty that person is, use temperature ratings as a general guide, keeping in mind your own internal thermometer.

Deciding between a down and a synthetic bag depends on your budget and the climate you plan to use it in. Down is more expensive than synthetics, yet it is more compressible for packing, lighter weight, and more durable. With repeated compression, a down bag will retain its loft about twice as long as a synthetic bag. The newer synthetics are making advances in compressibility and light weight, but still cannot compete with down's longevity. The advantages of a synthetic bag are 1) it costs less, 2) it will retain some insulating value when wet, 3) it will dry quickly in the field, and 4) it is easier to clean (see Chapter 12). A soaked down bag can take days to dry, and offers no insulation. If you plan to hike in wet climates, such as the Pacific Northwest, a synthetic bag is your best choice. Where rain and humidity are less of a concern, a down bag will give you the best value.

The great disadvantage of down—that it won't work when wet—can in part be overcome by the use of Gore-Tex. For outdoor clothing—and a sleeping bag is basically a garment—people have long wanted a fabric that would not let rain in but would let out the moisture that the body gives off. You have noticed that if you wear a coated nylon garment, you soon feel clammy and wet—that's your body *moisture* condensing on the inside of the garment, even when you aren't sweating. If a sleeping-bag shell were made of such material, it would trap your body moisture, and before dawn the down would be rather moist and hence not a good insulator. Gore-Tex and other similar fabric treatments are being advertised as the long-wanted waterproof-breathable fabric, and are being used in making sleeping bags, tents and outdoor clothing.

Gore-Tex is good for keeping light dew, snow, and condensation that occurs inside a tent from soaking through your sleeping bag, but a Gore-Tex sleeping bag won't replace a tent for protection from rain and heavy dew. Moisture will seep through the seams, and prolonged exposure to water can soak the bag.

If a down bag with Gore-Tex is beyond your budget, or you will be camping in wet places, choose a mummy-shaped sleeping bag filled with some synthetic material. Since synthetics do not compress as much as down, get the smallest synthetic bag you can possibly sleep in.

Buying a small down bag for a young child is very expensive unless successive children will inherit and use it, so for children the best choice usually is a synthetic-filled mummy bag.

When shopping for a bag, test the zipper to see that it slides easily and does not tend to catch the interior cloth. Then try sliding the zipper from inside the bag. Also try tightening and loosening the hood drawstring, if the bag has one.

Most sleeping bags come in two sizes based on height, and most offer the option of having the zipper on the left or the right side. If two of you are shopping for sleeping bags you would like to zip together, mummy bags will work, as will non-mummy bags. Buy one with the zipper on the left side and the other with the zipper on the right side. The bags can then be zipped together side by side to create a double sleeping bag. To save weight, some manufacturers offer a single sleeping bag that, when opened up and zipped to a bottom, single layer of nylon, creates a very light weight and inexpensive sleeping bag for two.

Carry your sleeping bag in a *waterproof* stuff sack with a drawstring. (In wet climates use a plastic garbage bag also, to be doubly sure.) You can stuff it smaller than you can roll it, and the sack will protect your expensive investment.

When storing your bag, leave it loose—don't compress it.

What about a pillow? You can do without one; you can put your clothes or boots under the head of your sleeping bag or you can make a pillow by stuffing clothes into the sack that carries your sleeping bag. I carry a small zippered, cotton pillowcase and stuff my clothes into it. In bed, I wear a knit cap, which allows me to stick my head outside the bag, where it likes to be except on very cold nights. (If you keep your head inside the bag, your breath's moisture will condense in it.)

The Bed

What to put under your body is another story. Your weight, of course, compresses the filling of your bag until it is very thin, so you need something more between you and the cool, damp (and sometimes hard) ground.

At one time the most popular mattress was an inflatable air mattress, and some backpackers still use one, but most use a foam pad. Basically, there are two kinds—closed-cell and open-cell. A closed-cell foam pad (Ensolite is the commonest material) compresses much less than an open-cell pad, and is a better insulator. The common ½ inch thickness doesn't offer enough padding for real comfort if you sleep on your side. Open-cell pads come in thicknesses up to 2 inches, which is plenty for comfort. A closed-cell pad is impermeable to water and air, and hence is preferred

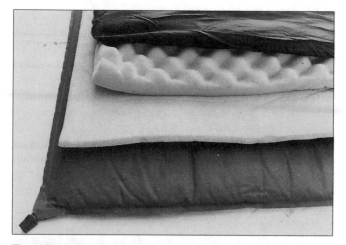

Top to bottom: nylon cover for open-cell foam pad, open-cell foam pad, closed-cell foam pad, Therm-A-Rest

by most for winter and wet camping.

Self-inflating air mattresses are another option for sleeping comfort. Therm-A-Rest, the most popular brand, consists of open-cell foam covered by airtight, coated nylon. While these are much more expensive than other foam pads, they offer excellent insulation and comfort. They do require extra care in keeping the valve free of dirt and preventing punctures. Although they are tolerable to sleep on when deflated, carry a patch kit in case of puncture.

Whether you choose an air mattress or a pad, you have a choice of lengths, from 6 feet down to about 3½ feet. Naturally, you should choose the shortest one you are comfortable on. That may be one that reaches only from your shoulders to your hips. I like some padding under my head, but below my knees the bare ground, my empty pack or some clothes is usually enough.

Most children and some adults sleep comfortably with no mattress to give softness, so long as they don't get cold from contact with the ground. If you are one of them, you can, in warm weather and at low altitudes, dispense with a mattress and use just a plastic sheet, to protect your sleeping bag from dirt and to keep out the dampness of the soil.

Before you buy a pad, lie down on it in the store. They won't mind. On your trip you will be sleeping on ground just as hard as the store floor, or even on rock.

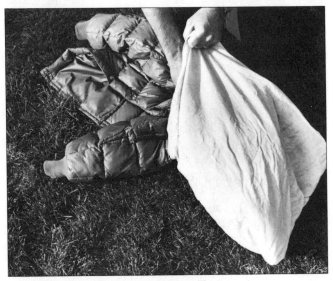

Stuff pillowcase with clothes to make pillow

The Tent or Tarp

Unless you're willing to take a chance on getting soaked, or even freezing to death, you need a tent or tarp. Tents are expensive, tarps are cheap. Tents keep out the wind; tarps don't. Tents generally keep out the rain; tarps keep out some of it. Tents keep out insects; tarps don't. Tents give privacy; tarps don't. Tents keep you a lot warmer, tarps a little warmer. Tents weigh more. So you have some choices to make.

In recent years the weight of backpacking tents has been decreased considerably, so that the weight advantage of a tarp is less than it once was. A good wilderness tent that sleeps two or even three persons typically weighs about 4 to 6 pounds, including stakes, poles, ropes and rain fly. (A rain fly is a fitted, waterproof "umbrella" that goes over the tent body.) If you usually go

Lightweight 2-person tent (rainfly not pictured)

with a larger group, you might buy a 4-person tent that weighs 8 to 9 pounds with everything.

Backpacking tent designs have come a long way in recent years. Once all you could buy was a "pup" tent, a triangle in cross section with the ridge held up by a pole at each end. Now there are literally hundreds of shapes of tents. For convenience, we can classify them as follows: dome tents (also called free-standing tents) versus tents requiring stakes and/or guylines to stand, and 3-season versus 4-season tents. Dome tents, whether 3- or 4-season, come in a variety of shapes, but all are held up by poles under tension that arch diagonally across between opposite sides or corners. There are usually from 2 to 4 of these poles. Since dome tents require no stakes or guy lines to stand erect, they are very convenient, particularly in rocky areas where it is difficult to drive in stakes. They're also good to have when all you need is privacy or something to keep the mosquitoes away. In a big wind, a dome tent will require stakes and sometimes guylines to keep it from blowing away, and in the rain or snow to make the tent fabric taut enough for water to flow easily off the tent sides—and to give strength. Tents that *require* stakes in order to stand come in many shapes, from the A-frame design similar to the old "pup" tent to tunnel-shaped tents with arching poles.

3-person dome tent (rainfly not pictured)

These tents tend to weigh less than similar-sized dome tents, since they usually have fewer poles.

Three-season tents are tents designed for use in late spring, summer and early fall as compared with 4-season tents, which are strong enough to handle high winds and heavy snow. These added strength features in a 4-season tent make the tent much heavier and are unnecessary for most backpacking.

Whatever shape of tent you buy, the important things are the same: cost, size, amount of usable space, weight, water repellency, wind resistance, ventilation, quality of workmanship and ease of erection. Since a good tent costs so much, you should borrow or rent several kinds before you buy, and talk to tent owners about their experiences. When examining a tent, pay particular attention to how smooth and tight the cloth is when the tent is erected. Don't buy one that has a lot of wrinkles and sags; it wouldn't withstand brisk winds, let alone gales.

After you do buy, practice pitching your tent at home before you pitch it in the wilds, where it just might be windy, raining or dark. I have had to get out of bed on moonless nights and pitch my tent before a storm hit, and although I never did it with my eyes closed, I think I could have.

Gore-Tex, mentioned above in the discussion of bags, has also been used to make tents. These tents don't require a rain fly because the Gore-Tex bars rain but passes water vapor out. Gore-Tex tents are all right where there is plenty of ventilation and where temperatures stay above freezing. Below freezing, the water vapor inside the tent condenses and freezes on the inner walls. Once frozen, it won't pass through the material as water vapor will. There are other tents without rain flys, made of waterproof fabrics, but unless they are very well ventilated, water will condense on the inside walls and eventually get things pretty wet.

Once, campers typically *ditched* their tents, digging a trench around the tent to carry rainwater so it wouldn't flow under the tent and soak up through the floor. But now most tents have a waterproof material on the floor, which also runs about six inches up the walls, so you don't need to dig a trench. Besides, digging a trench would violate the minimum-impact ethic.

A tarp is a flat piece of material that is waterproof or nearly so. The cheapest tarp is one made of polyethylene sheeting, from 2 to 4 mils (thousandths of an inch) thick. More expensive and more durable is coated nylon. A poncho, which is a sort of raincoat, can double as a tarp in camp, because it can be laid out flat. Some plastic sheets, some ponchos and all coated-nylon tarps have grommets around the edges for tying cord to. Gadgets for tying to an ungrommeted plastic sheet are available in equipment stores, or you can push a small, smooth object into the tarp and tie a loop around the base of the "wart" you thus create.

Another inexpensive type of shelter is a "tube tent," a rectangular piece of plastic or coated nylon about 9 by 10 feet which has been formed into a tube by sealing together two opposite edges. When you string a taut cord through the tube about 3 feet above the ground to form a ridge, and unroll your sleeping bag inside to hold down the "floor," you have a tent of sorts that is open at both ends. With clothespins you can close the ends enough to keep out the rain during a light rainfall, and you can also pinch the plastic onto the cord so that it doesn't slump toward the middle of the slightly sagging cord.

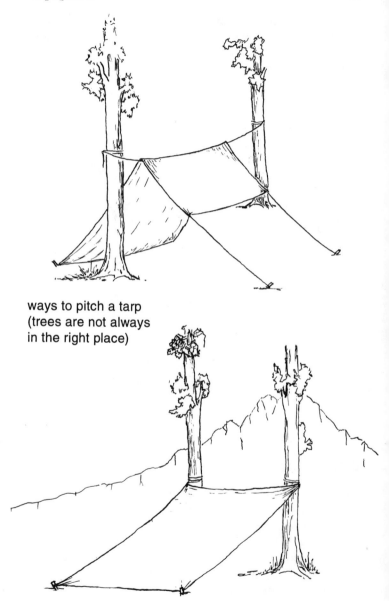

ways to pitch a tarp
(trees are not always
in the right place)

As to the merits of sleeping alone or together, people's tastes vary, but there's no denying that sleeping together conserves body heat better. That goes for two in a tent in two sleeping bags, or two in one sleeping bag.

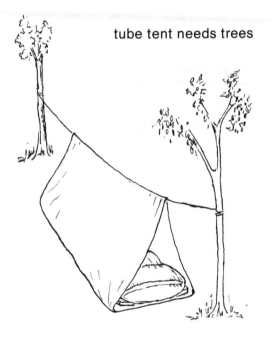

tube tent needs trees

Other Equipment

A *flashlight* is almost a must. Some experienced backpackers rely on getting their eyes adapted to the dark, and even walk on moonless nights. They have to avoid looking at even a match flare if they don't want to wait 30 minutes for their eyes to re-adapt. Lightweight flashlights are available that use two AA batteries. They weigh much less than those using C or D cells, give adequate light, and are much easier to hold between your teeth when you need both hands. A headlamp, which is basically a flashlight that straps to your forehead, is convenient for keeping your hands completely free while you make dinner, pitch your tent, or hike in the dark.

With any flashlight, you must guard against its turning on in the pack and thus running down the batteries. To avoid this, depending on the design of your flashlight, you can unscrew the bulb partway, reverse one battery, or tape the switch off. Two alkaline AA batteries last me through a one-week trip if I avoid using them except when I really need the light.

A *knife* belongs with every backpacking group, if not in every hiker's pocket. Many knives are gadgets and conversation pieces, and are too heavy for most purposes. You can spend up to $70 for a knife with 10 or 12 blades, including a corkscrew. But most of your knife use will be confined to the cutting blade or blades, and you might be satisfied with a simple, one-blade, good-steel pocket knife. The romantic image of the expert outdoorsman carrying a long hunting knife in a belt sheath is very out of date. Unless you are going to dress a deer in the wilderness, a 3-inch blade is long enough.

Too-big knife, good knife with belt attachment

Some kind of *water purification system* is required on almost all backpack trips. Earlier editions of this book said that "in true wilderness, the water is usually safe to drink." We can no longer say that because of the spread of the protozoan *Giardia lamblia,* which can be found even in remote lakes and streams. Drinking water infected with *Giardia* can cause a very unpleasant illness, giardiasis. Its symptoms are diarrhea, nausea and stomach cramps.

Fortunately, preventing giardiasis isn't too difficult, and there are several options. You can disinfect your drinking water by boiling it for at least one minute (at sea level—it could take 15 minutes at 10,000 feet). This method is quite effective for killing *Giardia,* though time consuming. You'll need to carry enough purified water for your hike (or stop to boil more as needed) and additional fuel in your already heavy pack. Disinfecting your water with iodine tablets is the lightest-weight method and is fairly simple. Disadvantages are that some people don't like the slight iodine taste of the water and you have to wait one-half hour for the disinfecting process when you use any iodine-type system. Iodine tablets lose their potency soon after the bottle is opened, so any tablets remaining after the end of the season should be discarded. Although iodine is recognized as quite effective against *Giardia,* there is some question as to the effectiveness of chlorine.

Filtration is another method you can use to purify your drinking water. There are several backpacking water filters available. Though somewhat-to-very expensive, they are convenient and provide good-tasting, clean water almost instantly. Filters available on the market are either of the disposable variety, which are less expensive, or the re-usable and cleanable variety, which are much more expensive in the short-term, but will last through many lifetimes of the disposable variety. If you buy or borrow one, be certain the filter's pores are small enough to remove *Giardia* cysts. The filter should be labeled effective against *Giardia*—2 micron screen. Even better is a 0.4-micron screen, effective against *Cryptosporidium.*

Since a pint of water weighs a whole pound, don't carry more than you need, as most beginners do. In early season in the mountains, rills and rivulets are everywhere. In late season, if you have some camel blood in you, you can go for several hours over easy terrain without getting too thirsty. I carry a quart Nalgene bottle but don't always fill it. I do make sure to keep it handy so I will continue to drink throughout the day to stay well hydrated (see Chapter 10, "Safety and Well Being").

Cord is useful for many purposes. Braided nylon ⅛ inch in diameter (parachute cord) tests out at over 500 pounds breaking strength, enough for a simple rescue. In bear country, you need 50 feet of it to throw over a tree branch so you can hoist your food out of harm's way (see Chapter 7). You will have tied enough cord to the tying places on your tent or tarp before leaving home, but in a big wind you might need an extra supply. Nylon cord is also good for erecting a tube tent, stringing a clothesline, making emergency repairs to pack or boot, and giving added security when you are fording a rushing stream. I carry 100 feet of cord, including the 50 feet for bears.

On short trips with a few people, you do not need a whole roll of *paper towels* or *toilet paper.* When the rolls in your house get down to the right size, put them away with the backpacking supplies.

A few other pieces of equipment are necessary, such as a first-aid kit, but these will be discussed in the appropriate chapters. See Appendix II for a checklist of equipment, clothing and supplies.

If you can't afford a lot of new equipment, look around for used equipment. Bulletin boards at mountaineering stores, colleges and other places often have good bargains, and stores specializing in used equipment are springing up. See also the classified ads in any magazine or bulletin that circulates among backpacking types. Check the latest imports. Some are reasonable facsimiles of American-made equipment at a lower price.

3

· · · · · · · · · · ·

Clothing

Use Layers

On some backpack trips you hardly need any clothes at all, but in the high mountains it becomes cool or cold at night, even in midsummer. It may freeze any night in the year. Your good down sleeping bag will defeat the cold once you go to bed, but as soon as the sun goes down (which may be as early as 3 P.M.) you will want to put on something warm. And unless you sleep very late, you will want to put on something warm in the morning. There may be entire days when you'll want to wear something warm.

What keeps you warm is an envelope of warmed, still air around your body. If air would stick to your body like molasses, you would be warm naked on Mount Everest. But air doesn't stick—it circulates. First, your body heats the air close to it, and this heated air rises and moves away. Then some cooler air flows in to take its place. So you need something to impede air movement. The thicker this something is, the thicker is your envelope of still air.

Naturally, when you're cold, you'll want to put on all the clothes you brought. By selecting these layers carefully, you can assure yourself of being warm and dry as efficiently as possible, which is vital when you carry every pound. The clothing layers are divided into four categories: long underwear, shirt and pants, insulation, and wind/rain shell. By adding or removing one or more of these layers, you should be able to get comfortable over a wide range of ambient temperatures and levels of activity: from working up a sweat hiking in cool weather to sitting around after dinner on a cold evening. Likewise, you'll be prepared for rain and wind.

Underwear

The underwear layer has seen a significant technological advance with the use of polypropylene (known as "polypro"). This fabric has gained great popularity because of its light weight and its wicking ability. Wicking is the process whereby polypro (and some other fabrics), when next to the skin, carries moisture away from your skin. Moisture is wicked to the outside of the garment, where it can evaporate without cooling the wearer as much as if it evaporated right next to the skin.

Polypro has disadvantages too. It retains body odor remarkably well, so after prolonged use it smells terrible. When washing it, you must avoid heat: use cool-water wash and no dryer. There are some similar fabrics that achieve the same wicking effect and don't have some of polypro's drawbacks.

Two natural fibers—silk and wool—also work for the underwear layer. The high price of silk deters many people from using it, though it works quite well. Wool can be uncomfortable next to the skin but it has the advantage of keeping you warm even when it is wet. Avoid cotton for active pursuits in cold weather, as it will chill the body when any moisture in it slowly evaporates.

Clothing

The next layer outward is the clothing layer. This can be any of a variety of articles of clothing, preferably something absorbent that will help draw moisture through the underwear layer to where it can evaporate away from the skin. This layer is usually the long-sleeved shirt and long pants—or shorts—you'd wear in mild weather. More on that later.

Insulation

The third layer is the insulation layer. Here your choice of garments can vary considerably according to your personal preference, your budget and the temperatures you expect to face. If you don't expect very cold temperatures, the possibilities include . a wool sweater or one of the newer synthetic pile or fleece jackets. I prefer a jacket that zips up the front for easy ventilation and easy removal. The advantages of pile and fleece jackets are that they are lightweight, keep you warm when wet, and dry quickly. These jackets are expensive compared with an old wool sweater you may already have or can buy cheap at a thrift store.

If you expect cold temperatures or get cold easily, you will need to supplement this layer with an additional sweater or vest, or use a warmer jacket. A down jacket is a lightweight option that offers warmth and protection from wind. You must not get it wet, or it will become almost worthless for keeping you warm.

As with sleeping bags, the nearest equivalent to down-filled garments is synthetic-filled garments. Heavier filling is required to confer the same amount of warmth, but synthetic garments don't lose much of their warming ability when wet. They also cost less than comparable down garments.

Rainwear and Windwear

Finally, you have an outer shell to protect you from wind and rain. Whatever stops water stops wind. You want an outer layer that will keep you dry in the rain and warm in the wind. Until recently, any garment that was totally impervious to water would keep all the rain out, but it would get you very wet by keeping your body vapor and your sweat in. Now you can buy an outer garment made of nylon coated with Gore-Tex or another water proof but breathable fabric. As noted earlier under "Sleeping Bags," Gore-Tex presumably keeps out rain but lets out your body vapor.

Waterproof-breathable fabrics work because they have very tiny pores. Water in its liquid phase won't fit through these pores, but water vapor (a gas) will fit through them. There is a limit to the breathability, however, since some of your body moisture condenses before it reaches the Gore-Tex. Leakage can be a problem in Gore-Tex garments at the seams if they are not sealed (most should be factory-sealed with tape) or when the garment is dirty. The garment may also leak at pressure points like shoulders under straps and at the knees when kneeling.

Gore-Tex parkas are expensive. You can get by more cheaply with a poncho, which is so loose-fitting that it has many places for your body moisture to get out—and rain to get in.

**Rain parka   Poncho covers more,
with hood   flaps more in wind**

As for the style of the rain-wind garment, I wear a hooded Gore-Tex parka with full front zipper. Like all good mountain clothing, it opens down the front, so I can wear it open or closed to adjust the amount of heat retention. This style is also easier than a slipover to get into and out of. If I am pretty sure it will not rain during my trip, I save about ¾ pound by substituting for my parka a thin, uncoated nylon windbreaker. One attraction of my parka is the four large pockets in front and the one super-large pocket across the back. If my pack is too full, I can put some things in the pockets of the parka, which travels on top of the pack, ready for instant use if rain or wind comes up. And the pockets carry all I need for a day's hike away from base camp. Be sure you get a parka large enough to fit *loosely* when you wear it over all your other clothing. Also be sure it has drawstrings at the hood and waist, and some device for closing the wrists snugly.

Since skin dries quicker than clothing, I prefer to keep hiking in my shorts and t-shirt during a short rainstorm on a warm day, rather than stop, retrieve my raingear from my pack, and overheat while hiking with the raingear on. I stay plenty warm while hiking, and am no wetter than I probably would be with my sweaty clothes under raingear.

Rain pants are not a necessity, but during a downpour or walking through wet brush, you'll appreciate keeping your lower half dry. If your rain jacket is not long enough to cover your backside, rain pants are a must, to keep the water that's dripping from the bottom of your jacket from soaking your hiking pants. Rain pants also prevent the water that pours down your legs from filling your boots.

Think ahead to stay comfortable. Add layers before you get chilled and unzip or remove layers as you become active. Don't let yourself get all sweaty before you remove your jacket.

Vapor Barriers

Vapor barriers have been touted as an excellent way to stay warm and dry. Though the reasoning is sound, the idea hasn't caught on. This may be due in part to the uncomfortable feel of a waterproof fabric right next to the skin. Regardless, this is how it works:

If your skin weren't slightly moist, it would crack and bleed. Not surprisingly, the body has a built-in mechanism for keeping the skin moist. When triggered, this mechanism turns on the organs for making "insensible sweat"—which is water *vapor,* as distinguished from "sensible sweat," which is water. What triggers this mechanism?—the drying out of the skin, of course. Now, skin exposed to air dries faster than unexposed skin, but skin under a garment also dries out—unless the garment is vapor-proof. Breathable fabrics are not vapor-proof, and they allow body vapor to pass outward, into the surrounding air and also, of course, into the surrounding clothing such as a down jacket. As the vapor passes outward, the skin humidity starts to fall, so the organs produce more insensible sweat. The clothing is cool enough that the water vapor condenses in it. This water in the clothing makes it far more conductive of heat—20 times as conductive as dry air. So the garment you have put on to help you stay warm begins to conduct heat away from you at a rapid rate.

This whole process is accelerated when you are in cold air, because cold air is dry air. Being dry, it gobbles up your water vapor faster, your skin-wetting organs have to work faster, and more water condenses in your garments. (It also condenses in your sleeping-bag insulation when you are in the bag.) The water that condenses in the clothing eventually re-evaporates, when it has absorbed enough of your body heat to vaporize it. It takes 555 *times* as much heat to vaporize a gram of water as to raise its temperature 1°C and all that heat comes right from your body.

How to avoid this chilling? Vapor barrier theorists say you should wear, right next to the skin, garments that are absolutely impermeable to water. (Some allow wearing a thin layer of polypro under the vapor barrier to minimize its slippery feel.) They also recommend that in cold weather you wear plastic sacks on your feet under your socks, and cheap plastic painters' gloves on your hands.*

When you wear a vapor barrier, your skin stays moist even with very little output of insensible sweat, and none of it can get into your clothes. Hence your clothes stay dry and give you the maximum insulation they are capable of. On the outside, you can wear a *waterproof* garment because there's no need to let body

---

* Jack Stephenson of Warmlite Company enjoys telling how, in Vermont where he lives, he always carries a supply of plastic gloves when he goes skiing. When he encounters a skier with cold hands, he gives the person *one* plastic gove to wear under a ski mitt. Very soon, he says, the person notices the difference between the two hands, and approaches Stephenson to ask for a second plastic glove.

moisture escape. But since the barrier won't let water out, you can't afford to let yourself start to sweat profusely. Opinion among vapor-barrier theorists varies on how to solve this problem. Your options include ventilating through zippers under the armpits to let out heat, opening outer garments at the neck as soon as you notice any sensible perspiration, and removing those outer garments.

The opposite view, of course, is the breathability view, and it is still the majority view. Gore-Tex and other similar fabrics are merely the latest in a long series of answers to the question of how to let out our body moisture while barring the rain from coming in through our clothes. Breathability advocates say that when you wear a vapor barrier while exercising, as in backpacking, you are bound to nearly drown in your own sweat. I personally find it very hard not to overheat, even with underarm zippers, unless I remove some garments as I heat up. If it's raining, that presents a real problem, and of course you have to take your pack off to add or subtract garments. Nevertheless, I often use vapor barriers.

Vapor barriers in sleeping bags are more common than vapor-barrier clothes. It makes sense: when you're asleep, there's no problem of avoiding overheating and consequent sweating. A vapor barrier will add more warmth to your bag than an equal weight of additional down, and it eliminates the need to dry your bag before you pack it the next day.

Shirt and Pants

Fortunately, you don't need to buy high-technology shirts and pants. Because your clothes always take a beating in the wilderness, wear the toughest material you can get. If you may run into cold, wet weather, choose wool. Wet cotton can literally lead to death. The more pockets you have, the better. Choose a long-sleeved shirt that can be buttoned at the neck. It will protect you from the sun and mosquitoes. To cool off, unbutton the neck and the cuffs. To warm up or to avoid mosquitoes, button up.

Many hikers prefer short pants for walking, but short pants are silly in brushy country, and no help in mosquito land. Some hikers carry both shorts and longs, and some are switching to overalls.

On most trips, no change of clothing—except socks—is necessary. If anything gets so dirty or smelly that it bothers you or your companions, wash it and let it dry in the sun while you do other things.

Hat

I don't see why anyone would backpack without a hat. The mountain sun shining on your head can make you downright ill, and the desert sun can kill you. Unshaded eyes are subject to

their own painful version of sunburn. In addition, your poncho hood or parka hood, even though you put it up during rain, probably won't keep wind-driven rain out of your face and eyes, but a hat brim usually will. Finally, a hat is a garment you can use to cool off or heat up. For instance, on a hot day, push the crown up to create a larger dead-air space between your scalp and sun's hot rays. For bald people, a hat is an even better device for regulating temperature. Since about one third of the heat your body radiates is given off by your head, you can hold in a lot of heat by putting on your hat, or get rid of a lot by removing it.

Your hat should have a wide brim all around, as a barrier against both sun and rain, and it should be able to take a lot of hard use. Choose one with an ample crown, not a flat top. Give it some water repellency by spraying it with a repellent. But don't wear a waterproof hat; it won't let out the water vapor your head gives off, and your head will be drenched.

If you expect cold temperatures, bring along warm headgear too.

Bandana

Experienced hikers play the game of finding new uses for the bandana. Beginners know that a large bandana makes a good out-of-doors handkerchief, and then they see it can be a washcloth. It can also be a dishcloth, a towel, a pot holder, a scarf, a makeshift hat (knotted in each corner), a mosquito net for the face while napping, a sling for an injured arm, a tourniquet, a bandage, a food cover, a headband to keep hair and sweat out of eyes, an ever-ready rope for tying things, a wrapper for freshly caught trout, a visible warning tied to clothesline or tent guy-lines in camp so that people don't walk into them, a signal flag (if it's red), a swimsuit, and a carrying bag for side trips. For me it is everything but a towel; my towel is superabsorbent rayon.

Swimsuit

Oddly enough, some law of nature seems to be eliminating the need for a swimsuit just when one is becoming necessary. A few years ago, the wilderness hiker could usually find a private place to bathe, and didn't need a swimsuit. Now it is much harder to find privacy; however, many wilderness travelers' attitudes toward nude swimming are changing. You'll have to decide for yourself each trip whether you want to carry the few extra ounces of a swimsuit.

Of course, underwear works too.

Gloves

I strongly recommend a pair of cheap cotton gloves. When you are breaking firewood or moving fireplace rocks around, gloves minimize cuts and punctures. When mosquitoes are peskiest, gloves protect the back of the hand and the wrist. When it is cold, they give warmth. They also substitute for a potgrabber (see Chapter 4) and may weigh no more than one.

In colder seasons, take a pair of wool gloves instead.

Sleepwear

Sacrifice all else to stay warm and dry, have happy feet, and sleep well. If you need a pair of pajamas or a nightgown to sleep well, bring it. Most people quickly get used to sleeping in their clothes, their underwear or nothing.

4

• •

Food and Cooking

Even if you can't cook, you can cook on the trail. All you
need is some hot water and a package of freeze-dried food.

You can get many fruits, vegetables and meats in freeze-dried
form. When you add hot water and wait a few minutes, the food
is restored to something like its original condition. It tastes good
when you are trail-hungry; some of it you would even serve to
guests at home. The biggest drawback is the cost. Freeze-dried
food is expensive.

One step down from freeze-dried food, and as far down as
most hikers go, is dehydrated food—anything that has little or no
water in it. Such foods are widely available in supermarkets, and
they cost much less than freeze-dried foods. But many of them
demand more work to prepare. Dehydrated foods include old
standbys like uncooked cereals, newer creations like Lipton Cup-
a-Soup, and food especially made for backpackers, sailors and
others who find light weight and imperishability very important.
You can get most common vegetables and fruits, and some meats
and dairy products, in dehydrated form at backpacking stores or
supermarkets, or by mail from catalogs (see Appendix I).

For the more ambitious, home-drying your food is a possibil-
ity, from drying fruit or beef for snacks to drying entire meals
like curried chicken and vegetables with a first course of soup.
Home drying requires a lot of labor and time, but if you are con-

cerned about cost, have dietary constraints, or have a gourmet streak, this may be the alternative for you. Many cookbooks on food preserving have chapters on food drying to tell you how to do it. See Chapter 14 for further recommendations.

One more step down from dehydrated foods—some purists would call it a step up—is food eaten cold. It simplifies. If you can get used to eating foods that require no cooking on the trail, you will be way ahead of everybody else in convenience and in the hour that you start the day's hike. The no-cook breakfast and the no-cook dinner are like the lunches that most people already eat on the trail: dry salami, cheese, crackers, candy bars, nuts, raisins, fruit-drink mix (add water), powdered milk (add water). Even simpler than a meal of such things is a meal of one multipurpose food. Two common types of multipurpose food go by the names *muesli* and *granola*. In them is almost everything a normal person needs nutritionally for a week or so. One can draw on stores in one's body for the few vital things these mixtures lack.

Here is a list of some of the foods available in *freeze-dried* form. Most come already cooked. (See Appendix I for a list of suppliers.)

Freeze-Dried Foods

Fruits	apricots
	bananas
	blueberries
	fruit cocktail
	peaches
	pears
	pineapple
	plums
	strawberries
Vegetables	beets
	carrots
	corn
	green beans
	peas

Freeze-Dried Foods (continued)

Vegetables
(continued)

mushrooms
potatoes
spinach
tomatoes

Dairy foods

cottage cheese
yogurt
eggs

Drinks

cocoa
coffee
milk

Meat

beef dices
beef patties
chicken dices
crab
fish
ham
pork chops
meatballs
shrimp
beefsteak
turkey

Main dishes

beef stew
chicken stew
beef with rice
pork and potatoes
chili with beans
beef hash
chicken chop suey
turkey Tetrazzini
beef almondine
chicken with rice and carrots
shrimp Creole
beef chop suey
beans and franks
spaghetti in mushroom sauce

Now, here is a list of some *dehydrated* foods suitable for backpacking. Most are available in supermarkets. Others may be ordered from backpacking-supply stores (see Appendix I). Natural-food stores are also a good source of dehydrated and other dry foods.

Dehydrated Foods

Breads and cereals	Minute rice
	quick-cooking cereals
	biscuit mix, cornbread mix, etc.
	spaghetti, macaroni, noodles
	crackers
	Ry-Krisp, Finn Krisp, etc.
	ready-to-eat cereals
	wheat germ
	granola
Vegetables	carrots
	peas
	green beans
	corn
	onion flakes
	tomato flakes
	instant mashed potatoes
	hash-brown potatoes
	spinach
Fruits	apples
	currants
	raisins
	apricots
	peaches
	banana flakes
	prunes
	dates
	figs
Dairy foods	dry milk (whole, skim or butter)
	eggs
	cream substitute
	cheese

Dehydrated Foods (continued)

Meat and other	salami
protein foods	jerky
	chipped beef
	Canadian bacon
	nuts
	peanut butter
	tofu
	roasted soybeans
	lentils
Drinks	cocoa
	coffee
	tea
	soup
	juice drinks
	pudding
	jello
	fruit juice
Sweets	honey
	sugar
	candy bars
	hard candies
	marshmallows
	cookies
Flavorings	vegetable flakes: onion, celery, parsley, green pepper, etc.
	gravy mixes
	herbs and spices
	margarine
	salt, seasoned salt
	pepper
	bouillon

Suppose you've got enough money to buy all the freeze-dried food you want, and you have investigated what backpacking food is available. Then your menus for a weekend trip should, in my opinion, look something like this:

Friday dinner	fresh steak or other luxury
	instant mashed potatoes
	freeze-dried vegetable
	coffee, tea, milk
	freeze-dried or dehydrated dessert
Saturday	freeze-dried fruit or juice
breakfast	freeze-dried eggs (scrambled or om-
	elet, with meat if desired)
	coffee, tea, milk
	granola for those still hungry
Saturday lunch	salami, jerky, cheese, nuts, Ry-Krisp,
	dried fruits, candy bar, lemonade
Saturday dinner	dehydrated soup
	freeze-dried beef stew or other entree
	coffee, tea, milk
	instant dessert
Sunday breakfast	same as Saturday breakfast
Sunday lunch	same as Saturday lunch

The way to simplify kitchen work on the trail is to prepackage everything in advance, meal by meal. Use sturdy plastic sacks. Figure out how much of each thing (other than condiments and staples) you need for a meal. If any cooking or reconstituting directions are needed, cut them off the package or write them on a piece of paper and put it in the plastic sack with the food. Put all food sacks for one meal in one large plastic sack (some hikers prefer a cloth sack), and write on the sack what meal it is.

You can further simplify food preparation on the trail by doing as much preparing at home as you can. You can probably combine at home any dry ingredients that are to be cooked or served in the same dish—for example, cereal and dry fruit. Add dry milk in advance to pancake mix, biscuit mix, instant pudding, etc.; then, in camp, you need add only water. (Write on each package how much water to add. If you have added dry milk, use as a guide the directions for reconstituting dry milk.) If everyone in your party likes one teaspoon of sugar in coffee, mix equal parts of instant coffee and sugar in advance, to carry in a single bag.

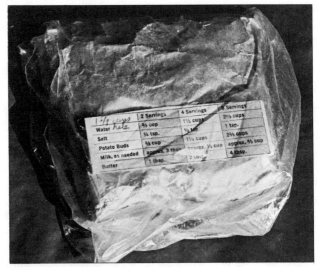

Food packed with cooking directions

How much food do you need? A general rule is 1½ pounds of dry food per person per day. Most people find they eat less than at home for the first few days on the trail, but begin to get very hungry after 5 to 7 days. So by the end of a week-long trip you might be eating 2 pounds a day. Pay no attention to the statement on any food label about how many people the contents serve. Try a dish at home to find out how many people it serves. Or else get an accurate little scale, and weigh things. If you plan by weight, you will have enough food overall, even if you have too much salami and too little Noodles Almondine.

What kind of food do you need? You need protein, carbohydrate and fat. Eat some protein at every meal—meat, milk, eggs, cheese, nuts, if you are not a vegan. It is especially important to have protein and fat for breakfast on a hiking day, as they give off their stored energy gradually, rather than quickly, as carbohydrates do. You should have your vitamins, minerals and bulk in fruits and vegetables, but the weight problem won't allow you to carry much fresh produce, if any. Freeze-dried fruits are good but expensive. Ordinary dried fruits can be eaten plain or stewed.

You can get your vegetables in dehydrated soups and stews, or you can buy dehydrated or freeze-dried vegetables unmixed with anything. Don't rely on fish or wild plants for any part of your food requirements.

Backpackers also need to drink lots of water. Hiking greatly increases a person's need for fluids to prevent dehydration, particularly at higher elevations and in the desert. Drinking lots of water can offset some of the effects of high altitude, as well as contribute to your general well-being. Plan on drinking at least two quarts of water per day. Hot drinks with breakfast and dinner are helpful. I enjoy hot soup with every dinner. While you're hiking, keep your water bottle handy and drink often.

Cooking Equipment

What do you cook your food in—if you're cooking? Perhaps no more than one pot, and certainly no more than three, will be plenty for any ordinary trip of not more than six hikers. While aluminum pots are the lightest weight, stainless steel pots designed for backpackers are also available. The larger pot should hold *one pint per hiker* or slightly more, and the others should be progressively smaller so all the pots will nest together. You need

A fully equipped kitchen

lids for the pots, to shorten cooking time. A good substitute for a pot lid is a piece of aluminum foil.

Whether you need a frying pan depends on what you will cook. The lightest frying pan is a cake pan. Some pot lids will double as frying pans. If you want steak the first night out, despite its cost and weight, you can omit a frying pan and barbecue the meat, if you carry a small grate (provided you'll be camping where a campfire will cause minimal impact). You can barbecue any fish you catch—though I much prefer fish fried in margarine or bacon fat. A frying pan is traditional and convenient for cooking eggs, whole or powdered, but these can be cooked in a pot just as well.

Although pot lids shorten cooking time, some dehydrated foods won't cook at high elevations even if you boil them all day, and everything takes flabbergastingly longer in the mountains. Dried beans are notoriously hard to cook. At 5,000 feet cooking time is doubled, and at 10,000 feet it is quadrupled. Precooked food avoids delay at high elevations.

To speed up measuring liquids in camp, scratch pint lines on the inside of your aluminum pots. In Chapter 2 I mentioned taking a knife. You'll need a pint poly bottle for mixing milk and juice. For a group of four or more, a quart poly bottle in addition will be very handy. If you will have to carry water any distance, a plastic water bucket is very convenient. The only other kitchen equipment you will need are a pot-grabber (but gloves will substitute), a fork, and one or two large spoons. I prefer plastic utensils, including the spoon, which are lightweight and won't scratch my pots. If you are cooking pancakes, you will also need a spatula. Each hiker should carry for himself a spoon, a plastic or stainless-steel cup, and a plastic bowl about six inches across. Any food that goes on a plate can go in a bowl, and you do not need a fork to eat with. Some hikers omit the bowl and eat from the cup, then drink from it later.

A recent innovation in outdoor cooking is the equivalent of an oven for backpackers. Using a heat diffuser and a hood, your pot with lid becomes a convection oven for baking anything from pizza to brownies. Meal preparation requires more of your precious time in the wilderness, but you're rewarded with an even greater variety of camp meals.

Wood Fire or Stove?

Now comes the basic question of whether to burn wood. Since man discovered fire, he has enjoyed sitting around a fire, especially in the company of people he likes, and especially after a good meal. Modern, urban man certainly seems to enjoy cooking on a bed of coals. But there isn't enough wood in the wilderness for everyone to use as much as they want. There certainly isn't enough for everyone to depend on having a campfire. In many places in the mountains, wood fires are now illegal. The lack of wood and the proliferation of unnecessary and unsightly fire rings resulting from overuse led to this drastic measure.

On evenings without a campfire, you may be more inclined to notice the wonders of nighttime in the wilderness. Viewing sunsets from a spectacular vantage point, taking a moonlit stroll, and star-gazing are far more compelling evening activities if you don't have a campfire holding your attention.

Obviously, the best choice is to depend on a small backpacking stove for cooking. A stove is cheap, it works without much trouble, and together with enough fuel for a weekend trip it weighs less than two pounds. On a backpack trip, human energy is very precious, and the energy you save not gathering and breaking up wood, and not blowing on the fire to make it go, may be greater than the energy you spend carrying those two pounds of stove and fuel on your back.

There are backpacking stoves that burn kerosene, ones that burn white gasoline (also known as Coleman fuel), and ones that burn butane or propane, which comes in a metal cartridge, or canister.

Kerosene stoves must be "primed" with a little gasoline or alcohol before the nozzle will vaporize the fuel. Most white gas stoves must be primed first, with white gas, and some newer models have a built-in pump to help this process. Stoves that burn butane or propane need no priming, so they are simple to light, but the fuel costs considerably more than white gasoline, it doesn't burn as hot, and butane performs worse as the temperature drops. Butane will not work at all below 31° at sea level or below 12° at 10,000 feet. Some cartridges must be empty before you disconnect them. Others can be disconnected anytime (hence you can take the cartridge to bed with you to keep it warm). Propane does work well when cold, but the cartridges are large and heavy.

You would not, I'm sure, leave used-up cartridges in the wilderness, so with the weight of the empty cartridges included in the carrying, you save weight overall by using a kerosene or gasoline stove.

I use an MSR Whisperlite stove, which is light weight, fuel-efficient, and quiet. It will burn for 4 hours on the fuel in the stove plus the fuel in the standard 1¼-pint fuel bottle I carry. You will probably need about ½ cup of fuel per day for 2 people (but take more the first time, to make sure). For each additional person, add 10% to the 2-person fuel ration.

If you buy a stove, be sure to practice using it at home first. Unless it is a propane or butane stove, you will have to prime it before it will start. To do this, you need some fuel in the cup at the base of the burner. If the stove has a pump, open the fuel valve and pump until a few drops run down into the cup. Then close the valve. If it has no pump, you can get some fuel out of the tank or our of your fuel bottle with a plastic eye dropper and put it in the cup, or—if your fuel bottle has a small pouring spout—you can pour directly. After making sure all caps are back on the bottle and the tank, light the fuel. When it has almost all burned up, open the valve a little. If you're lucky, the stove will start to burn. It may do so in spurts, but if you give it time, the burning will smooth out. If it doesn't start, go through the priming process again. Clean the stove's nozzle before using the stove each time.

Instead of fuel, you could use some solid fire starter to prime your stove.

All gasoline stoves are potentially dangerous. Use great care. In particular, don't let the fuel tank get too hot, or it may explode. Gasoline stoves have a safety valve, which, if it functions, will prevent a bad explosion, but you will still have a jet of flaming fuel to contend with. Avoid it by not overheating the fuel tank. Finally, never refill the stove while it is burning.

Regardless of what stove you're using, keep in mind that you want to carry and use as little fuel as possible. Use lids on your pots when heating and cooking, and shield the stove's flame from wind. Set up your kitchen in a sheltered place, and use the wind screen included with many models of stove, or position your gear to crate a wind screen.

When packing a gasoline stove, wrap stove and fuel bottle thoroughly so that gasoline cannot spill in your pack. Better yet, have someone carry the stove and fuel who doesn't carry any food. Nonfood things aren't much damaged by a spill.

If you've chosen a campsite where a campfire will have a minimal impact, another alternative to using lots of wood in a campfire is using a little. Build a very small fireplace of two rows of rocks with flat upper surfaces, the rows placed only about six inches apart. Your pots and pans will span the gap; you won't need to carry a grate, which is usually made of some heavy metal, unless you're going to barbecue.

keep fireplace small

Dishwashing

Now let us simplify your dishwashing in camp. If you sleep the first night beside your car—as I hope you will if you're hiking in the mountains, so that your body starts to get used to the lower oxygen content in the air at high elevations before you begin hiking—bring eating plates for dinner and breakfast which you can leave in the car. If paper plates haven't been outlawed by the time you go, they are the simplest. On the trail, I use no soap or detergent to wash my dishes, utensils, pots or pans. I wipe off any grossly excess food particles and boil everything in my largest pot. Before discarding the dishwater, I remove any food particles that might entice any wildlife. I've never got sick in the mountains, so my experience says this method of dishwashing is adequate. (You may find this method too unfastidious.)

Naturally I don't wash any dishes after eating breakfast on the day I walk back to the trailhead. That's done at home. And I wash the soot-blackened outsides of my pots and pans just once a year. You have precious little time in the wilderness. Why waste any of it scouring the soot off the bottom of a pot, when you can slip each pot into a plastic bag? Besides, a black pot absorbs heat from your stove or small cooking fire better than a shiny pot does.

Practice Runs

Just as you would try out your cooking stove at home and put up your tent in the backyard, I would advise you to cook every dish at home before you cook it on the trail. If you do that, you will find out in what ways life is different from what the directions on the package suggest. Then, before you actually cook the dish in camp, you'll be able to make adjustments. You'll also find out which backpacking "specialty foods" taste lousy to you.

To simulate camp conditions, you can turn off your home stove's burner for a few minutes, pretending that the fire went out while you were lingering by the stream watching the sunset colors, and you can try to make an instant pudding congeal in a refrigerator that you have set at 40° Fahrenheit. (It won't.)

5

• •

Day Hikes—A Prelude

Some people have been avid walkers all their lives, and have gone on literally hundreds of day hikes. They are probably more than ready to start backpacking, if they want to.

Other people have seldom if ever taken a hike of a few miles into the wilds. For them, a few day hikes can provide the experience that will make their first backpacking trip a pleasant and successful one.

A "training" day hike should be in an area where you also might backpack. You want to get the feel of being far from civilization, and you want to experience some of the same joys and the same discomforts as you would on a pack trip. On such a day hike, you will get practice in maintaining a steady pace, in fording streams, in resting the right amount, in always knowing where you are on the map, in keeping dry in the rain, in keeping warm in the cold, in everything except sleeping on the ground—and you could even do that for a while. You can cook a backpacking type of dinner for a midday meal, maybe once on a stove and once on a cookfire. You can take your tent and pitch it, maybe several times on different kinds of sites. You can carry a regular frame pack or a soft pack filled so that it weighs as much as it will on a real backpack, just to see how it feels over a few miles.

So if you want to start backpacking but haven't been dayhiking before, I strongly recommend you do that a few times.

53

6

• • • • • • • • • • • • • • • • • •

Planning Trips

Now that you have all your equipment and some idea of what to do once you hit the trail, you are ready to plan a trip. The planning breaks down into *who, what, when, where* and *how*.

Who

Since the choice of companions is so important, start with that. To begin, don't go alone. Solo wilderness hiking is only for very experienced backpackers, and even for them I don't encourage it. If you want to take your family on a backpacking trip but are unsure how well you yourself will make out, go with some other people first to gain confidence. Or perhaps you will go with your spouse to get a little experience before taking your children. If you have no family, and you won't feel embarrassed about your lack of experience—which you shouldn't—ask an organized backpacking group in your area whether they have a trip you can go on. Sierra Club chapters are the most obvious among many such groups. Generally, the people on a group trip will be at least adequate companions, because most of them will have had some experience.

Under "Who" comes the question of taking pets. Dogs are allowed anywhere in national forests but are discouraged in wilderness areas and forbidden on trails in national parks. I oppose taking a dog, but if you must take a dog along, remember that it may get cold at night if not in a tent, and try to crawl in bed with you. Remember also that rocky trails can hurt its feet and bears could kill it. Dogs are only visitors to the wilderness too. Keep your dog under strict control to prevent it from disturbing or harming wildlife. "Doggie packs," in which the dog can carry at least its own food, are available at some backpacking-supply stores.

A backpacking dog

What

If you are deciding what type of trip to take, keep it *simple*. Don't let yourself in for 200 miles of driving each way on a weekend. Plan on only a few trail miles per day—somewhere between 2 and 5 depending on the terrain. Limit the number of people to four or so. Even two is not too few. Choose a trip that is entirely on good trails. Allow plenty of time for each phase of the trip. Plan the simplest menu you can stomach. And as I said, don't depend on fish or wild plants for any part of your food.

Finally, don't plan a trip you won't be in shape for. Let's put it another way: get in shape to do the trip you'd like to do. That may require regular conditioning exercise for months in advance (see Chapter 8).

When

The answer to *when* depends on two things: whether you crave solitude, and when you will have time. If you don't want to see a lot of people on the trail, go between Monday and Friday, go before the Fourth of July or go after Labor Day—if your schedule will allow it. Many beginners who depend on the presence of others for a feeling of safety and security prefer to see a number of other people.

Whenever you go, you should allow at least two nights away from home. Getting up, leaving home, driving to the trailhead, walking to your campsite, making camp and cooking dinner all in one day is too taxing. For some people, the 3-day weekend every week is already here, and for the rest, it is on the way. Meanwhile, try to get away early enough Friday night to drive to the trailhead in time to get plenty of sleep. More adventurous backpackers may walk into the wilderness in the dark after eating dinner at the trailhead. If the moon is half full or more, they'll have plenty of light.

For me, *when* is September and October, because the High Sierra, where I go, is so unspeakably beautiful then and because the crowds are gone—except near trailheads on the opening weekend of deer season, which I avoid. In other Western mountains, where the fall rains—and the first snows—come earlier, October is rather late. I also like to go early in the season, sometime around late June, just after the ice has broken up on all but the highest lakes. The mountains then give off a marvelous feeling of awakening from winter—and the mosquitoes haven't yet hatched. Around the country generally, summer is the best time, but in the Southern states and in desert areas, summer is really too hot. More and more backpackers are breaking the summer mold and choosing the best time in their particular bailiwick.

above: an early trip when the ice has broken up on the high lakes

below: a late trip that experiences six inches of new snow

Sometimes the weather has a way of saying no to the best of plans. If official forecasts for the area you were planning to go to strongly predict a storm, you should either postpone the trip or drive up prepared to turn around if the forecast seems to have been correct.

Where

Despite the population explosion and the backpacking explosion, there are still plenty of places to go, and there will be for years to come. (Whether there will *always* be plenty of places to go is not nearly so clear. If it's important to you that the wilderness be preserved, get active in the fight to preserve it. Someone is always trying to carve off a hunk of it for mining, lumbering, resort building, or some other pecuniary purpose.)

You may decide to choose a trip from a guidebook. Wilderness Press guidebooks are the best there are. Or perhaps you will learn about a good trip from a friend.

Whatever itinerary you decide on, be sure everyone who is going understands the plan *and agrees to it.*

In planning where to camp each night, remember you can camp legally almost anywhere in a national forest, and you can camp happily anywhere that has the campsite attributes you desire. You can even camp where there is no water, if you carry enough.

How

How will you make the trip? In particular, what will you need, and how will you transport it to your destination in the wilderness? Some of what you need is in the closet where you keep your equipment. Some of it is on the shelves of supermarkets and the shelves of backpacking-supply stores.

Having decided who, what, when and where, you know pretty well how *much* equipment, food and supplies you will need, and you know how many people of what size and what strength are available to carry it all. So now it is time to make lists. Have each person make a list of all the equipment, clothing and supplies he needs for himself. (The list in Appendix II will get you started.) If you will be the trip leader, make a list of what the group will need, and check over the personal lists of the other people. All this is best done several days in advance, to allow time for having second thoughts and remembering things temporarily forgotten.

Prepare a menu for all meals, and after everyone agrees to it, make a list of all the food required for that menu. Buy it and prepackage it (see Chapter 4). Keep perishables in the refrigerator as long as possible. The night before you leave, assemble in one place all the packs and everything that is to go in them. (If you do this the day you leave, you are likely to do it so fast that you make mistakes.)

Divide things up so that each person carries their share. People often ask me, "How many pounds should I carry?" There is no flat answer—it depends on your size, your strength, your physical condition and the distance to be traveled. A strong person in good condition weighing 200 pounds can comfortably carry 50 pounds (25 percent of his body weight) for many trail miles. Most of us should not carry more than 20 percent of our body weight if we want to have a pleasant trip. If you are carrying extra fat on your body, you can carry even less weight in your pack.

When you put an item into a pack, check it off on the checklist. Pack heavy things close to your back and up high, so that they will ride as near as possible to your center of gravity. But make sure nothing hard (like the rim of a pot) is where it will dig into your back. If you have an external-frame pack, tie your sleeping bag, in its stuff sack, onto the packframe below the packbag. An ensolite pad will roll small enough to go under the packbag also; other pads may have to go under the top flap of your packbag.

When packing an internal-frame pack, take special care to keep the load balanced and the weight distributed properly. Start packing with all the compression straps loosened. Fill the bottom of the pack—or the sleeping-bag compartment if there is one—with your sleeping bag and clothing. You may want to retain your jacket to pack on top for easy access. Now add the rest of the load, putting the heaviest items where they will ride near your back, behind your shoulder blades. Distribute the weight evenly on each side to avoid being lopsided. I use assorted sizes and colors of stuff sacks to keep my things organized. Your rolled sleeping pad can be attached outside the pack with straps, or, if there's room, vertically inside the pack. I put my tent poles on the outside of the pack, lashed to one side. Without them, the tent body, fly and stakes are in a more manageable shape to fit in my pack or be

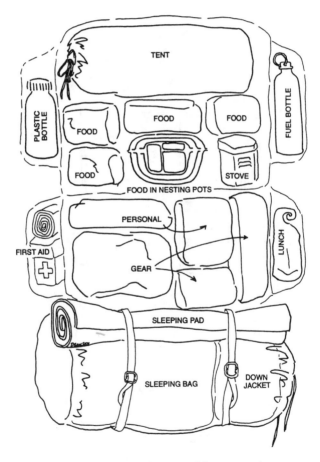

a well-ordered external-frame pack

apportioned among my companions. The top compartment is for items you want to keep handy: sunglasses, map and compass, sunscreen, etc. Once the pack is full, tighten the compression straps. This will compress the load and prevent it from shifting as you hike.

That is the ideal way to pack. But life is a compromise. For instance, one of your companions may live halfway to the

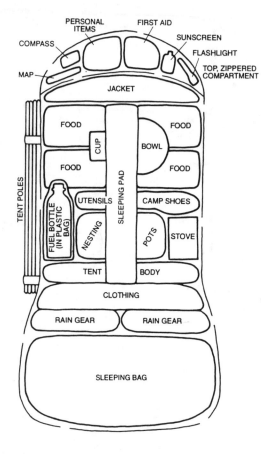

a well-ordered internal-frame pack

trailhead, and be unavailable for the community packing session. And you will probably be taking some food that should be kept cold until you hit the trail. You will keep it in the refrigerator until you leave home, and in a picnic cooler while driving. Don't forget to put it in your pack when you leave the car. Similarly, if you sleep the first night at the trailhead, you will have to pack sleeping bag, mattress, and a few other things in the morning. A last-minute search of your car will probably turn up anything you forgot to put in your pack. If you are taking a bus or train to the trailhead, or hitchhiking, you had better pack everything at home.

7

• • • • • • • • • • • • • • • • •

Trailhead Tips

Now you have all the equipment and food you need, and you are ready to go. I will skip over how to get to the trailhead, though it will probably be by car as public transportation these days is all too rare. (Some people call the trailhead the roadhead or the roadend. Whatever it is called, it is where you start walking.)

If you are going to elevations above about 5,000 feet, you should try to time your trip so that you sleep the first night at the trailhead, or near it. Up there, where the air is thinner, your blood makes adjustments so that it can continue to supply enough oxygen to your body, but making these adjustments takes time. If you drive from near sea level to 8,000 feet and immediately start walking, you are asking for trouble.

If you sleep by your car, you can have all sorts of luxuries there. You can have a huge polyurethane pad to sleep on, or even a folding camp bed. You can have a gasoline or propane lantern and a large stove. You can have whatever clothes suit your fancy. You can eat heavy, gourmet foods, and you can use all the pots and utensils you want to. All this is again true if you should sleep at the car after walking out of the wilderness, rather than driving home immediately. So take advantage of the fact that carrying an extra 100 pounds is a lot less tiring for your car than it would be for you.

In a large clothes bag I put the clothes and boots I will put on when I leave the car in the morning, as well as books, a swimsuit, and other things I may want to use while I'm with the car. This bag also contains clean clothes to drive home in. While I'm hiking, it contains things that are useless in the wilderness, like a wallet and coins. I carry just one quarter in case I need to make a phone call after an emergency exit.

Before leaving the car, put everything valuable out of sight and double-check that you have locked all the doors and windows.

Contents of author's clothes bag: hat, boots, hiking shorts, socks, underwear, credit cards, shirt, book, swimsuit

8

. . . .

Walking

Most people think that just because they were born into the bipedal human race, they can walk well. Not so—many people walk poorly and inefficiently. Between your front door and your garage it doesn't matter much, but on the trail it matters a lot.

If you're more than three years old, some of your walking habits are now impossible to change, but if you work at it you can learn at least two good hiking habits: start slowly, and walk rhythmically.

The story of the tortoise and the hare could have been written about trail-hikers. Those few hikers who are able to hold themselves down to a plodding pace from the very beginning eventually overtake all the "off-and-running" types, and are the first to arrive in camp. (Of course, I am not including comparisons of sixty-year-old desk-bound weekenders with twenty-five-year-old professional athletes.)

How fast you should go—your pace—depends on your body's strength, the load you are carrying, the distance you plan to cover, the time available to cover it, the steepness of the trail, the nature of the trailway and your mood that day. There is some trade-off between body strength and load. If you have exercised before your trip to get in shape, you can carry more pounds at a given speed; if you haven't exercised, you can go at that speed if you carry a lighter pack.

67

A person in poor physical condition can hardly carry any load at all, so it is important for you to condition your body in advance. Many Americans in their regular daily activities stay in good condition, but most do not. Those who don't must make the effort—and take the time—to exercise. The best exercise for hiking is running.

Walking is also excellent conditioning for hiking, but it takes much longer to get the same benefit from walking that you get from running. On the other hand, if there are nice places to walk near where you live or work, the pleasures of walking there make up for the extra time required. I find that when I'm walking along streets and roads where I have driven hundreds of times, I see many things I never saw before. Carrying a loaded pack while you take practice walks increases the benefits of the exercise.

Given your strength, your load, the distance, the time, the steepness and your mood, the proper pace for you is one that you can maintain hour after hour. Some people say that if you can't carry on a conversation you are going too fast, and I more or less agree.

The second requisite of successful hiking is a steady, rhythmic pace. You will need many miles of conscious practice before you can leave to your body the job of keeping in time with the March of the Happy Hiker. The tempo of this march varies: *andante* on the level, *allegro* going downhill, *lento* going up. Eventually the drummer who keeps the cadence in the back of your mind will learn to make the proper variations as needed. Sometimes a beat is syncopated, when just before landing on your forward foot you see a better place to place it, and you move it quickly there.

a happy hiker
in tempo

Going Uphill

Besides being in shape, there are a few tricks that make steep uphill walking easier. First, keep your foot flat on the ground as long as you can before rising onto your toes and lifting the foot forward. (This advice is also good for walking on the level, but more important going uphill.) Second, breathe in rhythm with your footsteps—two or four or six or eight steps per breath, depending. Third, when either your lungs, due to thin air in high elevations, or your legs, due to exertion, need rest, use the *rest step*. Advance one foot to a new position. Then lock the rear leg and relax the advanced leg. Pause a short moment. Finally, put the advanced leg to work again. The pause may last only a few microseconds, but it will do wonders for your ability to keep going. One final trick for steep uphill walking applies only to off-trail hikes; when the slope strikes you as too steep, start making your own *switchbacks*.

Going Downhill

It is disappointing that, after a stiff climb, you cannot simply put your gears in neutral and coast down the other side. But the fact is you have to apply the brakes. Going downhill is when blisters are most likely to develop, ankles to be sprained, toenails to be scrunched, and knees to turn to jelly. The defense against blisters and sprains is to tighten your boots, and maybe add a pair of socks. The defense against scrunched toenails is to cut them before the trip. The defense against jellied knees is to go slowly and take enough rests. Don't go so fast as to jar a headache into

step over, not on

existence, and don't have your advance leg absolutely straight when you shift your weight to it.

All the Time

Never step on a rock or a log if you can step over it. A broken leg or a sprained ankle in the wilderness creates major problems. Besides, it takes more energy to mount the obstacle, and the step down jars you more. (In rattlesnake country, of course, you won't put your foot down where you can't see.)

Rest Stops

How often should you stop, and for how long? Frequent short rests are the best, for a simple physiological reason. What makes your muscles tired is that they accumulate lactic acid, a chemical result of exertion. Two 5-minute rests per hour will decrease the lactic-acid concentration better than one 10-minute stop. Depending on all the things that affect proper pace, I stop for 3 to 6 minutes every 20 to 60 minutes. I also eat or drink something at every stop, be it only a lemon drop or a sip of water. Most beginners go far too long without eating or drinking.

You should not even start out until you are entirely comfortable, especially your feet and your back, where the pack bears on it. But even so, you will need a "shakedown" rest stop after about an hour, to adjust boot laces, pack, belt and clothing. This rest should last longer than 3 to 6 minutes, perhaps 20 minutes. On a hard day's hike, you will need several longer rests—besides the lunch stop—of up to 15 minutes. If they get longer than that, your body will cool off too much, and anyway long rests are a sign that you are going too fast.

After any stop, look around carefully for anything you may have set down and forgotten. Walking about 2 miles—a round trip of 4 miles—to retrieve a camera you hope is still there is well worth avoiding. It's best never to put anything down on the ground even for "just a second" if you have a pocket, sheath, loop, or whatever to put it in.

Up to now in this chapter you have been walking alone, but that will seldom be true. Since different people march to different drummers, some will *seem* to be stragglers. The leader or the deputy should go last, to make sure everyone gets to camp, but no one should criticize anyone else's pace or bow to criticism of their own pace. Finally, don't tailgate. There's plenty of room on the wilderness highway, and people go there to get away from the overcrowding of the city.

Having considered your physical needs when walking, now consider the effects of your feet on the landscape. On a trail, your passing will have very little effect; off-trail is where damage begins. The effect of walking one time across untrammeled ground may seem negligible, yet it can take years for plants and soil to recover from your steps, especially in arid areas, at high altitudes, on steep slopes, and in meadows. Footsteps damage plant foliage and roots, compact the soil, and invite erosion on slopes. One trip across a sensitive area may encourage others, seeing your footprints, to follow, leading to an unnecessary and damaging new trail. Even your footwear makes a difference, as a heavy-soled boot makes a deeper gouge in the earth than a lighter boot. The conscientious hiker will not shortcut trail switchbacks, will try to walk on rock instead of plants, and will avoid meadows and wet areas when possible. When crossing a sensitive area in a group, spread out instead of following one behind the other, to disperse the impact of your passing.

9

● ●

Camping Techniques

Choosing a Campsite

Now that you have been walking for six hours, you'd like to find a campsite. If you have already selected a trip from a Wilderness Press trail guide, you probably have tonight's destination in mind. Or you may have planned your trip yourself, using the principles discussed in Chapter 6. The features most people consider in choosing a campsite are listed below, not necessarily in order of importance.

    view
    water supply
    wood supply
    ground cover
    dead trees and limbs that might fall
    potential rock fall
    bedsites
    weather probabilities
    nighttime temperature at your bedsite
    probable wind direction and intensity
    exposure to morning and afternoon sun
    ecological considerations
    kind of soil and rock around the fireplace site
    swimming
    fishing
    recreational and educational opportunities nearby
    pest problems
    degree of remoteness
    man-made conditions versus natural ones
    general feel of the area

No campsite in the world is right on all these features, but quite a few are right on more than half, and where you choose to camp depends on which features are more important to you. These considerations, moreover, will vary with the time of year. If you like to catch fish but haven't done well yet this year, you'll be especially eager to camp near the shores of some water where you believe the trout are biting. If it's early or late in the season and the night might get too cold for you, you will want to camp up on a bench a few yards from the lowlands, where the minimum temperature may be 10 degrees higher. If you have seen too many people on the trail, again you will want to camp where you'll find solitude and perhaps a better view as well.

On the other hand, an already-developed campsite may have a fireplace, level bedsites and places to sit. In addition, the last person may not have used all the wood he brought in. So if you are especially tired, a much-used campsite will seem quite attractive. And you don't have to dismantle it the next morning in order that no one will know you were there. More and more, highly used campsites are permanent fixtures in the wilderness. But if you are going to build a fireplace that blackens some rock, and level a place for a bed where no one, as far as you can see, ever slept before, *it is your responsibility to remove all evidence that you* did *camp there*, so that the next hiker will find the place as much a part of real wilderness as you did.

When given a choice between a well-used site and a spot that has been used only once or twice, choose the well-used one. Evidence of your passing will be negligible compared to the more vulnerable slightly used site, which could recover if left untouched.

Of course you will not have constructed a house, shack or lean-to of limbs and boughs because you know they belong in the history books with the pioneers.

Water

Being near a stream shortens the water-carrying chore, of course, and it also gives you the nicest of all wilderness sounds to go to sleep by and wake up to. Being near a lake only shortens

the walk for water. If you like to fish or swim, the third virtue of camping near water is obvious. Unfortunately, almost everybody wants to camp beside water, so campsites there are by far the most used. As a result, camping is prohibited within at least 100 feet of many lakes and streams. Ah, well, the music of a large stream is quite loud enough even several hundred feet away. Besides, by conscientiously choosing your campsite, you'll be doing your part in preserving these lovely and fragile areas.

Exposure to Wind

In the mountains, wind is both good and bad. When the weather is hot or the mosquitoes are swarming, you want at least a breeze. When it is cold or stormy, a wind is piercing. Places where the wind often blows heavily in the same direction are indicated by lopsided trees—more foliage on the downwind side. Much more common than strong prevailing wind is daily change of wind di-

wind blows
left to right

rection: the wind blows *up* the canyon during the day and *down* the canyon at night. If you want to minimize the wind in your camp at night, pick a place in the nighttime lee of a grove of trees or behind large boulders. Orient your fireplace with the day-night wind shift in mind.

Exposure to Sun

Since nights are cool or cold in most backpacking country, you will enjoy beyond words a warm morning sun shining on your just-up, sleepy body. A campsite at the east or southeast edge of a stand of trees will be bathed by welcome morning sun but shaded from the hot afternoon sun. If the night will be cold, don't camp outside the trees, but just at the edge, for the trees hold in some of the day-gathered heat all night long.

Cold

Since cold air sinks, hollows are colder than the slopes above them. If you study plants to learn which ones like warmth the most, you can find the warmest spots in an area by finding those plants.

Runoff Channels

A rainstorm of any size will feed many freshets, and you don't want to be camping in their runoff channels. In addition, low spots can fill with water, creating small lakes. If there are some channels and low spots in the campsite you choose, at least don't locate your kitchen, your campfire or your bedsite in one of them.

Dead Limbs

The dead tree limbs you see on the ground were broken off by wind or by the weight of snow. Don't camp right under a tree that has any dead limbs which you think might come down in a high wind.

Making Camp

Now that you have selected your campsite, you are eager to reconnoiter, rest, fish, take pictures, or talk. Do none of these yet. Do what must be done.

First, remove your sleeping bag from its stuff sack, shake it to restore its loft, and spread it out. Then choose a spot for your kitchen area. A large, flat rock with places nearby to sit, or a similar log, seems to be ideal. I like to keep the view potential in mind when choosing my kitchen area. If you're planning to build

just right for morning

a fire, unless the campsite is an established one, you must choose a kitchen area where your fireplace will have the minimum impact. Gathering wood and making the fireplace, or rearranging the existing one as needed, is part of preparing the kitchen area, which is the next step. See "Building a Campfire" for details.

Next, lay out the dinner food and cooking utensils near the fireplace. Keep as much food (and nonfood) as possible in your pack, and keep each thing always in the same place in the pack. Dedicated "filing" will not only keep things where you can locate them immediately; it will keep them clean and unbroken, and safe from little animals. Animals, of course, need food, including salt—which they may try to get by chewing your boots or your fishing-rod handle. Furthermore, some rats and some birds like to take away shiny things, and yet other animal predilections, still unexplained, lead to what humans call "theft."

Now, locate your bedsite. If you are really tired, which is likely on your first trip, you will think that you could sleep on a bed of nails. It's true you could *go* to sleep on such a bed, but after a few hours you would regret not having made yourself a better bed.

So choose a level spot. If the best spot is not level enough, build up the low end; don't excavate the high end, for that would leave your torso sleeping on bare, damp earth, and would create scars in the earth which you would have to repair before leaving. If it's impossible to make a level bed, put your head uphill. Pick up all little rocks, twigs, etc., which might press up through your foam pad or puncture your air mattress. You don't have to pick up every pebble, but if in doubt pick it up. In any event, don't have a hump under your body. In fact, a slight trough where you lie is even better than a flat surface.

Now, pitch your tent or other shelter where you have chosen your bedsite. You will have practiced pitching your tent at home, so it should go up easily. On warm nights, when I want to sleep under the stars, I use the body of my tent, unpitched, as a ground cloth so I don't have to carry one to keep my sleeping bag and pad clean. Don't string cord where people are bound to walk— or, if you have to, at least tie something white to it, so everyone will see it, even after dark.

If your tent site is too rocky to allow using stakes to pitch your tent, you can still use your tent. Attach cord to the tent's stake loops and tie them off to large rocks. Use rocks light enough to carry, but heavy enough to hold the tent in a wind without losing tautness. This method allows you to pitch your tent anywhere, even on solid rock, provided there are enough loose rocks available. Remember to replace these rocks where you found them when you break camp.

To pitch a tube tent, see Chapter 2. How you pitch a tarp depends on how many people will be under it; what trees are around, if any; how hard the wind is blowing, and from what direction— among other things. Basically, you will have to think about it, and then improvise.

Now, one chore remains before cooking and eating—preparing your food storage system. Do it now so that after dinner you can easily hang up your food, cooking utensils and *fragrant* personal items like lip balm and toothpaste. This is most important in bear country, but you should also be wary of smaller mammals looking for treats in your pack and gnawing holes in your gear on their way in. These small mammals may also nibble at your pack and sweaty clothes looking for salt from where you perspired.

Because of bear problems in some backcountry areas, managing agencies have installed tall poles, cables and bear-proof containers not only to protect backcountry users' food but also to protect the bears. Once a bear learns to associate humans with an easy meal, it may become a nuisance, requiring its relocation to another area. This is disruptive to the nuisance bear and neighboring bears. In the worst case, the bear is destroyed. It is the wilderness users' responsibility to protect themselves and the bears with correct food storage techniques.

Most people hang their food from a tree limb, but a really smart bear can get almost any hanging food. Hence, if possible, use either of two surer methods. The first is to put your food on a high ledge. Bears can't climb steep cliffs. If there are no high ledges around, or if you are a poor rock climber, look for a deep crack in a large boulder. The crack should be less than 9 inches wide and at least 4 feet deep. Use a stick to push your food sack beyond a bear's reach, and in the morning lift the food out with the same stick. Just be sure you don't make your food irretrievable by you.

Lacking ledges and cracks, use the *counterbalance method* of hanging food. Find a sturdy tree limb at least 20 feet up. (In some national parks, the authorities have installed cables, which you can use instead of tree limbs.) Put your food in two sacks. Then follow the procedure outlined in the captions of the diagrams below.

If you have done it right, both bags will be at least 9 feet off the ground. In the morning you can push up one sack until you can reach the other.

If a bear does get your food, don't try to take it back! He will guard it as his own.

These bearbagging methods are also effective against raccoons.

A recent invention is the bear-resistant container which backpackers can carry in their pack. Weighing under three pounds, it can store about 3–5 days worth of food. At night, place the container far enough from your sleeping site so the bear won't be startled by waking campers. The bear needs time—about 10 to

Tie one end of the parachute cord to a rock and throw it over a limb or cable. If a limb, rope should be 8 feet from trunk.

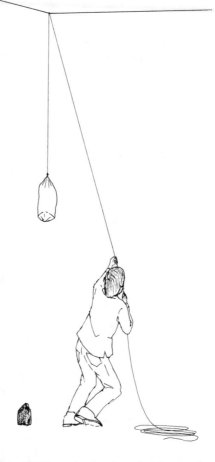

Untie the rock and tie on the heavier food sack. Then hoist the sack as high as you can.

Tie the lighter food sack onto the cord, as high up as you can reach. Two persons make this step much easier. Stuff all remaining cord into the food sack.

With a stick, push the lighter sack up until it is as high as
the heavier one.

20 minutes—to discover it is not a food source. These containers can be rented in some of the more bear-prone areas, and are required in a few of the most notorious bear areas. If you plan much hiking in bear country, these bear-resistant containers are available for purchase (see Appendix I).

If you happen to be camping in grizzly country, bear-bagging is essential not only to ensure your food supply but for personal safety as well. Items to put into your bearbags include all your food; cooking utensils; chapstick, lotion, toothpaste, and other non-food but "sweet" smelling items; and any clothing that had food spilled or wiped onto it. Don't underestimate the bear's ability to sniff out the most obscure items that it may think are food.

All bears are potentially dangerous. It is important to follow these precautions so that a bear, with its excellent sense of smell, won't be tempted to investigate your "sweet" smelling campsite. In its search for food, it may discover you in your sleeping bag. Careful camping techniques can prevent your own injury as well as the unnecessary destruction of a bear that's become troublesome.

Building a Campfire

If you build a campfire, you should not leave a trace of it. If there's an established fire ring where you camp, use it. If you want to build a fire ring, any of the following methods will ensure minimal impact.

Flat Rock Method: Carefully gather enough clean mineral soil to cover, several inches thick, an area slightly larger than the fire will occupy. Spread the soil on a flat rock—if there's one large enough—or on exposed bedrock and build your small fire. Don't ring your fire with rocks, as they would be permanently blackened, and if you really need rocks to support your grate or pots, use only a few and replace them where you found them when breaking camp. Burn all the wood completely. When the fire is out, crush the ashes, mix them with clean mineral soil, and scatter this mixture. Then remove the soil base and rinse the rock. There should now be little trace of your fire.

Pit Method: From an area about 12 by 24 inches, remove the sod or topsoil in chunks down to where there's only mineral soil, no organisms. Neatly arrange the chunks so they'll be easy to put back when you break camp. Remove all burnable materials near the pit and cover the sides of it with underlying bare soil to prevent drying of the surrounding vegetation. Moisten the vegetation if it shows signs of drying. Build your fire in this pit and be sure to burn all wood completely. When breaking camp, follow the same procedure with the ashes as above. Replace the soil and sod you removed from the pit, to re-create the surface as it was before you cut into it. Landscape the area with leaves, twigs, or whatever originally covered the ground.

Surface Method: If there is plenty of bare mineral soil available without excavation, you won't need to disturb the topsoil by digging a firepit. As with the flat-rock method, simply spread several inches of carefully gathered mineral soil over the area where you'll build your fire, and make your fire as usual. Burn all wood completely, crush remaining coals, mix them with clean mineral soil, and scatter. The campfire area should look undisturbed when you've removed the soil base and landscaped the area.

In areas with established fire rings, try to make as little impact as possible. Build a small fire, and completely burn all wood. Don't enlarge the fire ring. Leave the area looking more natural than when you found it. If there is more than one fire ring in the area unnecessarily, take all but one apart, scattering the ashes, rocks and "furniture" that's been moved around the fire ring. The wilderness experience of later visitors depends on visitors taking responsibility for maintaining or restoring the area's pristine quality. Being a conscientious fire builder is part of that responsibility.

How you gather wood depends on whether there is plenty of dry wood. If there is, gather from the ground enough wood of various diameters, and break it all into fireplace lengths, before starting the fire. Gather only *down* wood—fallen wood. Even if purists protest, use some paper as kindling. (For use in the fire next morning, keep your paper covered against the nighttime dew.) On the paper put some pine needles, if any are around. On the needles put twigs, up to ⅛ inch in diameter. You want the whole to be as loosely packed as possible. Now light it. When it is burning, add larger and larger pieces until you have the fire you want. Don't smother the little flame by adding wood too soon. But do blow on the base of it with a steady air stream to supply oxygen, and do shelter it from gusts of wind.

If the wood where you're camping is damp from recent rain or snow, look under fallen logs and in the shelter of boulders for enough kindling to get the fire going. As a last resort, and only in emergencies, break off dead wood from the lower trunk of a live tree. (The reason I say "last resort" is that breaking limbs off a tree, even dead limbs, is bad conservation practice.) With your knife, cut slanting notches into sticks that are not wet clear through to allow the flame to reach dry wood. Again using paper, pile the kindling loosely and proceed as you would with all-dry wood. If you have brought a candle, its flame will help get the fire going. Once you have a healthy fire, you can dry out more wood by piling it near the fire.

If rain threatens at night, cover the wood supply with a plastic sheet, held down by rocks.

Sleeping Warm

In a *good* sleeping bag, you will be warm on a cold night even if you err in locating your bedsite. You can also get away with going to bed in damp clothing, such as the underwear and socks you sweated in on the trail, but if you have clean ones, put them on.

In only a *fair* sleeping bag, you will have to be more careful. First, keep the bag *dry*. Second, keep it well fluffed up when it's not in your pack. As soon as you make camp, shake out your bag.

Having fluffed your bag, you can do some other things to ensure warm sleep. First, don't go to bed hungry or thirsty. You need fuel to stay warm. If your sleeping bag has no hood to pull over your head, wear some kind of knit cap or even a balaclava. For cold feet, start with dry socks. If that doesn't warm them up, put a plastic sack inside each sock. If your whole body is still cold, put on more clothes. You can also use your water bottle

filled with hot water to warm you. If all that fails, get up and look
for a warmer spot for your bed. Your (and my) natural inclination
is to stay in bed and hope to get back to sleep, but it's better to get
up. The warmer spot may be one in denser trees, one a little higher
up the nearby slope, or one farther from that snow bank. If you
have a tent you didn't put up yet, that warmer spot will be inside
it. And, as I mentioned in Chapter 2, sleeping together is usually
warmer than sleeping alone.

The Toilet

One of the biggest problems created by the increase in backpacking is sanitation. Except in far reaches of the back country,
one cannot be too careful.

If there is a constructed toilet where you camp, as there now
are at many wilderness campsites, use it. If not, copy the cat. Go
at least 100 yards from water, trails and camp, somewhere off the
beaten path, and dig a hole at least 6 inches deep. To dig, use
your heel, a stick, a rock—or a plastic trowel, which I carry for
this purpose. After using toilet paper, burn it completely in the
same hole. If you're in a fire danger area, pack it out. This practice avoids the "flags" of toilet paper one sees all too often in the
wilderness, and also helps keep down flies. Finally, cover the
results. Urinate in a similar place.

Breaking Camp

As soon as you are up in the morning, spread your sleeping
bag out to air. Inevitably, some of your body moisture is in the
bag's filling, and moist air would make bad insulation the next
time you used the bag. (If you have to pack before sunup, dry
your sleeping bag at the lunch stop, or at the end of the day's hike
if that will be early enough for it to dry.) If your tent is at all wet,
spread it out to dry. Actually, drying your tent before you pack it
is not necessary if you will re-use it the next night, though it will
be heavier. But if the tent is wet and will remain packed for several days, it could be ruined by the mildew that will form.

Consolidate all your garbage. Don't leave anything, even kitchen scraps.

If you built a fireplace, dismantle it as described in "Building a Campfire." You might even choose to dismantle a fireplace you didn't build.

Now, remove, obliterate and eliminate all other signs that you have been there, insofar as that is possible. Be creative in restoring the site. Scattering a few pine needles here and there, and brushing out your tracks will give the next visitor that same sense of solitude and wildness that you enjoyed. If you have treated the campsite respectfully, there will be little for you to do. If you have not, no amount of effort can restore the site to its former condition.

The last thing to do is to look all around carefully for anything you may have forgotten. There's usually something. Five minutes is not too long to spend looking.

10

• •

Safety and Well-being

Since the point of going backpacking is to enjoy yourself, you don't want to get sick or injured. Prevention is better than cure, and most emergencies are preventable; but you should be prepared for them. You will need a first-aid kit and some knowledge of first aid. But just as you do not memorize the recipes of all the things you cook, or the lines on the map where you're going, you don't need to memorize the contents of a first-aid handbook. Instead, carry one in your pack. Chapter 14 lists several good ones. Be in good health and physically fit before you start. You should also obtain and maintain immunity against tetanus, typhoid, and any deadly diseases of the particular area you are going to.

First Aid

Make up a first-aid kit to take along that meets your own needs and know how to use it. Later, as you gain experience, revise it to reflect what you have learned. Any first-aid kit should probably include:

  aspirin or ibuprofen for light pain and headaches
  codeine or other prescription for severe pain
  a laxative
  a disinfecting ointment for cuts and burns (such as Neosporin)
  band-aids (assorted)
  moleskin (for blisters)
  triangular bandages (2)

scissors
gauze pads for covering larger wounds
adhesive tape (2 inches wide)
a needle for removing splinters and piercing blisters
tweezers for removing splinters and other foreign matter
water-purification tablets
soap for washing wounds
sunscreen
ACE bandage
your personal prescriptions
paper and pencil (to record problem and treatment for medi-
 cal personnel to look at)

If your first-aid kit is in camp and you have an accident two miles away, it won't be much help. Carry it, always.

Prevention

To prevent illness on your trip, avoid getting too tired, drink plenty of water, and eat good food. A simple measure of whether you are drinking enough is the color of your urine. If the color is clear to light yellow, you are hydrated; if it's dark, drink more.

To prevent injury on your trip, don't take chances, especially near the end of a long hike. Don't try a daredevil climb on rock or snow unless you are an experienced climber with proper equipment. Be very careful of your footing when walking downhill, especially with your pack on. Be respectful of fires, knives, stoves, fishhooks, tent stakes, etc.

The commonest illness backpackers have is mountain sickness, which some people get if they drive rapidly up from near sea level. The cause is too little oxygen in the air you breathe, and the symptoms are headache, nausea, vomiting, fatigue, shortness of breath, palpitation of the heart, and diarrhea. If it is severe, the cure is to descend to a lower altitude; if mild, lie down and endure it till your body gets acclimated to the high altitude. However, you can avoid mountain sickness—if you happen to be prone to it—by sleeping one night in the mountains before starting to hike, not hiking too fast, and drinking plenty of water.

The commonest injury to backpackers is sunburn, because the burning power of sunlight is so much greater through the thin, clear air at high elevations. The badly burned person feels so terribly miserable that super-caution is justified to avoid this situation. Even if you have a good tan, don't rely on it for protection in the mountains, as you would at sea level. Whatever parts of you are not shaded by a hat and clothing must be covered with a rather thick layer of a good sunblock reapplied as necessary. If you are hiking around a lot of snow, multiply this advice by ten.

Your eyes are also subject to sun damage, and most people need sunglasses for long walks in the high country. Everybody needs them above timberline and around snow.

Poison oak and poison ivy are hazards in low elevations in some states. You can avoid contact if you learn to recognize them, and you can prevent the itchy rash by washing thoroughly with any ordinary soap soon after contact. In tick country, periodically check your clothing for ticks.

where not to be during lightning
1. under a tree or other tall feature
2. exposed on a high place
3. on wet, marshy soil
4. in the open

Bad Weather

If really bad weather strikes, seek shelter or turn back. Should the bad weather include a lightning storm in your immediate vicinity, stay off exposed places where you would be taller than your immediate surroundings. A safe place is among the smaller trees in a forest. If possible, stand on a dry, nonconducting object. Remember that wet things conduct electricity. Get rid of your camera, packframe, knife, belt—anything with metal.

In ordinary bad weather, the two things to keep are your spirits up and your sleeping bag dry. It's hard to remain ecstatic if a long rainstorm keeps you tent-bound for several days, but a few good books or a chess set can at least keep your mind occupied. Veteran backpackers in rainy climes consider books or games a necessity. As for a dry sleeping bag, you will survive naked in it even if *everything* else you own is soaked.

Hypothermia

Every year you can read accounts of hikers freezing to death in the mountains. They die of hypothermia, the #1 killer of outdoor recreationists. Because it is so easy to die from hypothermia, I am including the following information, which is endorsed by the Forest Service and by mountain-rescue groups. It may save your life.

Hypothermia is subnormal body temperature, which is caused outdoors by exposure to cold, usually aggravated by wetness, wind and exhaustion. The moment your body begins to lose heat faster than it produces it, your body makes involuntary adjustments to preserve the normal temperature in its vital organs. Uncontrolled shivering is one way your body attempts to maintain its vital temperature. *If you've begun uncontrolled shivering, you must consider yourself a prime candidate for hypothermia and act accordingly.* Shivering will eventually consume your energy reserves until they are exhausted. When this happens, cold reaches your brain, depriving you of judgment and reasoning power. You will not realize this is happening. You will lose control of your hands. Your internal body temperature is sliding downward. Without treatment, this slide leads to stupor, collapse and death. Learn the four lines of defense against hypothermia.

Your first line of defense: avoid exposure.

1. *Stay dry.* When clothes get wet, they lose most of their insulating value. Wool and pile lose less than cotton or down.
2. *Beware of the wind.* Wind drives cold air under and through clothing. Wind refrigerates wet clothes by evaporating moisture from the surface.
3. *Understand cold.* Most hypothermia cases develop in air temperatures between 30 and 50 degrees. Most outdoorsmen simply can't believe such temperatures can be dangerous. They fatally underestimate the danger of being wet at such temperatures. But just jump in a cold lakelet and you'll agree that 50° water is unbearably cold. The cold that kills is cold water running down neck and legs, cold water held against the body by sopping clothes, cold water flushing body heat from the surface of the clothes.

Your second line of defense: terminate exposure.

If you cannot stay dry and warm under existing weather conditions, using the clothes you have with you, *terminate exposure.*

1. *Be brave enough* to give up reaching your destination or whatever you had in mind. That one extra mile might be your last.
2. *Get out of the wind and rain.* Build a fire. Concentrate on making your camp or bivouac as secure and comfortable as possible.
3. *Never ignore shivering.* Persistent or violent shivering is clear warning that you are on the verge of hypothermia. *Make camp.*
4. *Forestall exhaustion.* Make camp while you still have a reserve of energy. Allow for the fact that exposure greatly reduces your normal endurance. You may think you are doing fine when the fact that you are exercising is the only thing preventing your going into hypothermia. If exhaustion forces you to stop, however briefly, your rate of body heat production instantly drops by 50% or more; violent,

incapacitating shivering may begin immediately; you may slip into hypothermia *in a matter of minutes.*

5. *Appoint a foul-weather leader.* Make the best-protected member of your party responsible for calling a halt before the least-protected member becomes exhausted or goes into violent shivering.

Your third line of defense: detect hypothermia.

If your party is exposed to wind, cold and wetness, *think hypothermia.* Watch yourself and others for hypothermia's symptoms:

1. Uncontrollable fits of shivering.
2. Vague, slow, slurred speech.
3. Memory lapses; incoherence.
4. Immobile, fumbling hands.
5. Frequent stumbling; lurching gait.
6. Drowsiness—to sleep is to die.
7. Apparent exhaustion, such as inability to get up after a rest.

Your fourth and last line of defense: treatment.

Victims may deny they're in trouble. Believe the symptoms, *not* the patient. Even mild symptoms demand immediate, drastic treatment.

1. Get the victim out of the wind and rain.
2. Strip off *all* wet clothes.
3. If the patient is only mildly impaired:
   a. Give patient warm drinks *only if fully conscious.*
   b. Get patient into dry clothes and a warm sleeping bag. Well-wrapped, warm (not hot) rocks or canteens will hasten recovery.
4. If the patient is semiconscious or worse:
   a. Try to keep patient awake.
   b. Leave patient stripped. Put patient in a sleeping bag with another person (also stripped). If you have a double bag or can zip two together, put the victim between two warmth donors. *Skin to skin contact* is the most effective treatment. Never leave the victim as long as they are alive. To do so is to kill them—it's just that simple!
5. Build a fire to warm the camp.

Being Lost

What about getting lost? Chapter 11 will tell you how not to get lost, but suppose you get lost anyway? First, sit down and think. When were you last on familiar ground? Where was it? You may find you aren't lost. If you are, think about how to help rescuers find you, and how to stay well. If you stay in one place, you're more likely to be found and less likely to exhaust yourself. You'll need water much more often than food. Save your energy for shouting periodically, making a fire, keeping warm and—as a last resort—walking out of the wilderness in the direction you finally decide is best.

Minimum Safety Package

There is a minimum safety package for use in the wilderness: waterproof matches, map, compass, a little food, rain gear, a warm garment, a whistle, a knife and a first-aid kit. I always carry these things, even when I leave my pack to make a side excursion. I've never been lost, but if I ever get a little confused, these things will be most handy.

The Right Companions

In my experience, the greatest threat to well-being and safety is the wrong companions. A backpacking group is a very intimate group. For everyone's well-being the hikers *must* cooperate extensively, and for everyone's safety, they must all be careful, prudent and helpful. Choose your companions very thoughtfully. Then, show the way in cooperating. Be extraordinarily considerate of everyone else. Offer someone else the first everything— serving of food, choice of bedsites, drink at the spring. By doing so you help build good will and group spirit that will overcome the interpersonal frictions which are bound to arise.

As for social relations with other people you encounter in the wilderness, remember that some love to talk, but some want to be left alone. Give the other person lots of room unless he invites you closer.

Drying Out

The backpacker's darkest moment comes when he is wet and tired and it is still raining. Of course, I have tried with my advice to keep you dry, but I may have failed.

If so, you have three choices—unless symptoms of hypothermia appear. You can walk back to civilization, you can be stoical about your plight, or you can stop and make camp. If you have good rain shelter, set it up quickly and stay in it with your pack until the rain lets up. No matter how skillfully you set it up, however, some water will probably get into it—another reason for being stoical. When the rain stops, make a fire, using the method described under "Building a Fire" in Chapter 9. String a line near the fire on which to hang your wet clothes and watch carefully in order to get the clothes dry without burning them. If you're lucky enough to have sunshine soon after the rain, use that instead to dry out. Think about how to avoid getting soaked next time.

Blisters

Blisters are easy to prevent but hell if they develop. If your boots fit well (see Chapter 2) you probably won't get blisters unless you allow your socks to get wrinkled or too dirty. Even then, you can prevent a blister by stopping *the very second* you feel any irritation. Don't wait until it hurts. Apply moleskin or plain adhesive tape to the irritated area and walk on. If you get a blister nevertheless, drain it only if it is too painful. Sterilize a needle, clean the skin around the blister with soap and water, and puncture the blister at the edge. Gently press out the fluid and cover the area with a dough-nut shaped piece of moleskin which you create with scissors. On a large blister, it may take several layers of moleskin to create enough height to take the pressure of your boot off the sensitive area. Leave it on until it comes off by itself. The blister will take days to heal.

If you are prone to blisters, carry a change of socks and wash them every day. You might also cut down on your mileage.

Mosquitoes

If you have no protection against mosquitoes, they can ruin your trip. However, protection is easy. Any insect repellent containing *N, N diethylmeta-toluamide* will keep them off. Don't buy one without it. Clothing is also a bar to mosquitoes—a good reason for wearing long pants and long-sleeved shirts. If you are a favorite target for mosquitoes (they have their preferences) you might take a head net—a hat with netting suspended all around the brim and a snug neckband. Planning your trip to avoid the height of the mosquito season is also a good preventive.

Stream Crossings

In early season, when the snow is melting, crossing a stream can be the most dangerous part of a backpack trip. Later, ordinary caution will see you across safely. If a stream is running high, you should cross it only if 1) the alternatives to crossing are more dangerous than crossing, 2) you have found a suitable place to ford, and 3) you use a rope.

As for #1, obviously it's better to turn back than to risk accident. As for #2, it may take considerable looking around to find a suitable place to ford. If you can find a viewpoint high above the river, you can better check out the river's width, speed and turbulence, any obstructions in it, and the nature of its bottom. As for #3, there are several ways to use a rope. The three diagrams below show the use of a continuous loop of rope with a minimum of three hikers. The first person crosses while the rope is tended by the second and third. They do *not* tie the rope to themselves. If the person crossing slips, the downstream person will haul them in. Never try to pull in a person upstream. Then the second person crosses, as the rope is tended by the first and the third. If the second person slips, the downstream person hauls them in. Finally, the third person crosses, with the same provision for hauling. If the group has a climber's sling and a carabiner, all but the first can cross while clipped to the rope and wearing the sling.

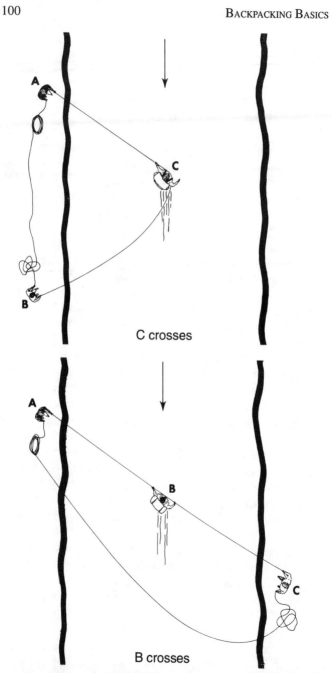

C crosses

B crosses

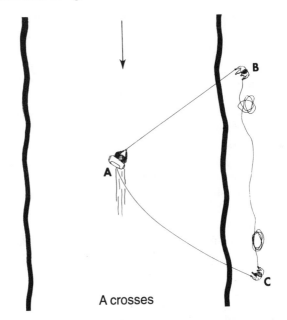

A crosses

These devices are described in *Basic Rockcraft* (see Chapter 14). The best rope for fording is about 150 feet of 5-millimeter climbing-type rope.

If the ford is not highly dangerous and you have no rope, two or three hikers should cross together, linked in such a way that only one need move at a time. One linkage is to form a circle with arms about one another's shoulders. Another way is one behind the other, facing upstream, with hands on the chest of the person in front.

Whichever method you use to cross a stream, you should:

1. If the water is at all high, wait till morning to cross, when the level will be at its daily low.
2. Unfasten the hip belt of your pack, in case you have to jettison it.
3. Keep your boots on. They will protect your feet from injury and give your feet more secure placement.
4. Never face downstream. The water pushing against the back of your knees could cause them to buckle.

5. Move one foot only when the other is firmly placed.
6. Never allow your legs to cross; keep them apart.
7. Use a stick as a support on the upstream side.

Wilderness Permits

The law requires you to obtain a permit if you are going into certain federally designated wildernesses in national forests and national parks.

You may write for a permit to the government official in charge of the wilderness area, stating where you are going and when. You may be asked to tell where you will camp each night—but if so, you won't be arrested for deviating from your plan! You may also secure your permit at a ranger station near your trailhead. In some national-forest wildernesses, permits are needed for day hikes as well.

Leaving Word

Good safety practice requires that you leave a copy of your itinerary with a relative or friend back home. Then, if you don't return on time, they can contact the authorities (if you've left the phone numbers), who will know where to look for you. To avoid unnecessary worry, *always* notify them immediately upon your return.

11

• •

Map and Compass

There are whole books on how to use a map and compass, but no one ever learned how entirely from a book. You have to *use* them in the field. All I can do is get you started.

The only kind of map I consider worth carrying in the wilderness is a topographic map ("topo" map). This is a government map, prepared by the United States Geological Survey, which shows not only lakes, streams, roads and trails, but also relief—the hills and valleys. It shows relief by means of contour lines—lines that are a constant elevation above sea level, like high-water marks on a reservoir that has been drawn down. In mountainous areas, where backpacking involves a lot of ups and downs, I consider the contours essential.

You can get topographic maps for most of the United States at a scale of 1:24,000, which is about 2.6 inches to the mile. These are sometimes called "7½-minute" topographic maps because each of them covers an area of 7½-minutes (⅛ degree) of longitude and 7½ minutes of latitude. The area within a Geological Survey map is called a quadrangle. In the latitude of Central California or North Carolina, a 7½-minute quadrangle is about 7 miles east-west by 9 miles north-south. Farther north, the east-west mileage is less because a degree of longitude becomes shorter in miles as you go toward the North Pole.

Once you learn how to use a topographic map and a compass, you can't get lost. If you were parachuted down somewhere in the mountains and given the topographic map of the area you were in, you could pinpoint your location—provided there were some distinctive landforms in sight—and you could walk to any other place on the map.

Before you start your trip, buy the topographic map(s) that covers it. Get your map at a backpacking store or by mail from the U.S. Geological Survey.

Distribution Section
U.S. Geological Survey
Federal Center
Denver, CO 80225

On the map, find your trailhead and your route. Study the surrounding country on the map to get some idea of what it is like. Then fold the map to a size that will fit your pocket, and put it in a plastic sack or envelope to keep it clean and dry.

After some experience you will know about how much distance—horizontal and vertical—you can cover in a day. You can measure miles on the topographic map by estimating or by using a map wheel, which you can get at a backpacking store or a map store for a few dollars. Since the map doesn't show the trail's small irregularities, the trail on the ground is longer than the trail on the map. To approximate true mileage for mountainous country, add to the length of trail on the map, as measured by the wheel or as estimated, 20 percent of the distance where there are no switchbacks and 100 percent of the distance where there are switchbacks. To determine the number of feet of ups and downs, count the contour lines that your route crosses and multiply by the contour interval, which is always given on the map.

How long will it take to walk the route you have planned? A rule of thumb that works out for many though not all backpackers is:

1 hour of hiking for every two horizontal miles
1 additional hour for every 1000 feet of ascent or steep descent

For example, if your day's plan is to walk 6 miles, and the destination is 2,000 vertical feet above the start, it will take you 3 hours + 2 hours = 5 hours. This formula allows for normal rest stops.

The main reason for having a compass is to *orient* your map—to position it so that north on the map is north on the ground.

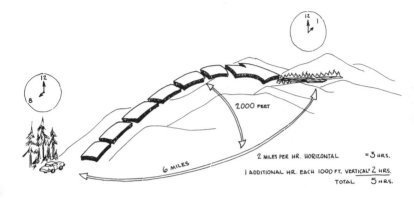

2000 FEET

6 MILES

2 MILES PER HR. HORIZONTAL   = 3 HRS.

1 ADDITIONAL HR. EACH 1000 FT. VERTICAL = 2 HRS.

TOTAL   5 HRS.

First, place your compass on the map with north on the compass pointed toward the top of the map. Then check the *magnetic declination* shown on the bottom margin of the map. For instance, in the High Sierra the declination is roughly 17 degrees east of north. In other words, in the Sierra your compass needle will point about 17 degrees east of true north. To orient the map, rotate the map,

Topographic map oriented with compass

with your compass on it, until your compass needle points 17 degrees east of true north.

Once you start hiking, check the map every mile or so to see where you are on it. Compare the map with what you see around you. Soon you will discover how a feature of the landscape, such as a peak, looks on the topographic map. You will discover that where contour lines cross streams, they make arrowheads pointing upstream. You will discover that where there are cliffs, the contour lines on the map are very close together. Eventually, you will be able to look at any part of a topographic map and get a pretty good idea of what that area actually looks like—if you practice.

When you can match map and actual terrain in your head, you are never lost. Using your compass—sometimes even without using it—you can choose and follow a route from A to B that you think would be interesting, or perhaps even easier than the trail route.

One other habit is very helpful in finding one's way around the wilderness. It might be called "hindsighting." As you hike, periodically turn around and look *back* at the country you have passed through. When you retrace your steps, the memory of these glimpses will help guide you.

A Forest Service map supplements a topographic map by (usually) showing more recent trail alignments than the topographic map shows. Alas, the Forest Service map also shows more recent logging roads.

Finally, a good road map will help you in driving to the trailhead. There are no perfect road maps, but those of the American Automobile Association and its state affiliates are the best. Do not, however, rely on them for roadless areas.

12

....

Equipment Care

As frugally as you may buy your equipment, altogether it will cost quite a bit. If your funds are not unlimited, take good care of your gear. First, use it correctly and gently. Second, keep it in good repair. Carry duct tape for making emergency repairs on the trail.

Check over all your equipment soon after bringing it back from a trip. Don't wait until you are planning the next trip, because then there may not be time to fix problems you discover. The shoe-repair shop sometimes takes three weeks to fix boots.

Sleeping Bag

Air your bag and then store it in a dry place, either on a hanger or piled loosely. Once a year or so, clean it. If you know a reputable commercial cleaner of down bags and clothing, you can take your bag to them. Be sure they don't use solvents that can harm down. To clean a down sleeping bag (or a down garment) yourself, wash it in lukewarm water in the bathtub or a large basin with soap specially formulated for down—not detergent. Gently squeeze suds through the bag, scrub stains with a soft brush, and then rinse thoroughly. Press out as much water as you can, then carefully lift the bag out to drip dry. Be sure to support the bag when you lift it, as the weight of the wet down could otherwise tear the inside baffles of the bag. Starting with a clean sheet under the bag and using it to lift the bag works well. Put the bag somewhere outside, preferably in the shade, where it can be generously supported. Allow the bag to air-dry until it is almost dry. This can take one to four days. Then put it in the dryer on the "no heat" setting with a couple of tennis balls or clean sneakers. Spin until it is completely dry and lofted back up.

Synthetic bags are easier to clean. They can be either hand- or machine-washed using a commercial, front-loading machine. Use cool water and mild soap. Synthetic bags dry quickly, and can be air-dried or machine-dried on the "no heat" setting. Never dry-clean your down or synthetic sleeping bag.

Gore-Tex Rainwear

Gore-Tex works best when it's clean and new. Cleaning Gore-Tex garments is simple. Just machine-wash, with two rounds through the rinse cycle. You can revive your aging Gore-Tex jacket by spraying it with ScotchGuard. This will increase its water repellency the same way the factory repellency treatment did when it was new, and not harm its breathability.

Boots

Check your boots for scratches, cuts, and dents in the reinforced toe and heel areas. If they're wet, stuff them with newspaper to help them dry. Glue down any loose flaps of leather. Fill any deep gouges with epoxy. Place a thick, damp cloth over any dent and apply a hot iron over it. Clean the boots well and apply a wax-base leather conditioner (for example, *Sno-Seal*). Once a year, or oftener, clean them very thoroughly and apply three coats, one a day, of silicone-base conditioner (for example, *Shoe Saver*). Your boots will hold their shape and not curl up at the toe if you store them with boot trees inside.

Cooking Utensils

The cooking utensils came home dirty, remember. Wash them well—though you don't really need to scour the black off the

outsides of pots. Renew the pint-mark scratches inside if necessary. Put the utensils away in clean plastic sacks.

Knives

Clean, sharpen and coat lightly with oil. If you fish, sharpen
your hooks at the same time.

Pack

Check your packframe for breaks in the metal fittings and the
main metal tubes. Check your packbag for rips in the fabric and
breaks in the zippers. Fix any questionable places.

Tent

To clean and thoroughly dry your tent after each trip, first
shake out the accumulated leaves and pine needles. Then clean
small stains with mild soap (not detergent) and a sponge. If the
tent is very dirty, hand-wash it in the bathtub with mild soap and
rinse it thoroughly. Air-dry your tent in a shady place. Avoid prolonged exposure to sunlight, because ultraviolet light damages
the nylon. Never dry-clean or machine-dry your tent.

Check the tent fabric and its mosquito netting for holes, and
patch as necessary. Seal the floor seams and rain fly seams if you
had problems with leaking. Never wear shoes in your tent. The
hard soles will weaken or tear the floor's fabric.

Check the tent poles for weakened or broken spots. Being sure
to fully engage the pole sections during assembly will prevent
most joint failure. When disassembling shock-corded poles, start
by folding them in the middle. The shock cord will last longer if
it doesn't get stretched to its limit each time. Replace weakened
or broken poles.

A common tent failure is due to a worn-out zipper slider. If,
no matter which direction you slide the zipper slider, your zipper
stays open, chances are that is your problem. With a little pa-
tience and a pair of pliers, you can revive your zipper for a few

more trips. First, see whether all the zipper teeth are in good condition. If not, the whole zipper will need replacement. Now, assuming the zipper teeth are O.K., slide the zipper slider all the way to the end, where you would normally move it to open the zipper. It may take a little force to open the zipper all the way, but don't overdo it and tear your tent. Now gently squeeze together each pair of wings of the slider, but not too close together. If you squeeze too hard, it won't slide and may crack. Now, test your revived slider. Good luck.

Emergency Items

Replace any emergency items you used on the last trip, such as penicillin pills or fire starter.

Personal Items

After the personal things you always take are washed, checked out, cleaned or replaced, put them all in a box ready to go into your pack the next time. Once you develop the habit of putting things where they are sure to get packed, you can dispense with a checklist for them.

Clothing

Carefully check your hiking clothes for holes, rips, missing buttons, and incipient failure. Replace any item that you're not sure will last for another trip.

13

Taking Children

Not to take your children backpacking could be called a cruel and unusual punishment, for certainly children love to camp out. Equally, that parent is deprived who never has the chance to watch their fascinated children watching a ground squirrel scurry around in the grass of an alpine meadow.

Although I don't think children are miniature adults or any other modification of adults—adults are unfortunate modifications of children—it will simplify the discussion of taking children if we add to the topics that already make up chapters of this book certain advice that pertains to taking children.

Getting Started

How old should the child be? That depends on how you feel about the matter. A month-old child, lovingly and patiently cared for, can thrive in the wilderness. How much the child enjoys it the child doesn't say, but loving parents enjoy having the child. For most people, however, a child still in diapers presents slightly too many problems. Some people who are not big, strong or dedicated would rather wait until the children are old enough to carry their own equipment. When you have read this book you will be better able to decide when to take your child, especially if you have actually taken a trip.

Equipment

If you are wealthy, you can buy all-new equipment for your children. Otherwise, you will have to give them a few makeshifts and hand-me-downs. In fact, hand me *down* is the only way most families can afford to furnish their children with down-filled sleeping bags and jackets. One of each will last for several years of use by each child, as he or she in turn grows into it. The same is true of the pack. But children should have real packs by the time they are 10 if you expect them to carry very much load—say, one quarter of their body weight—very far—say 5 miles. Until then, a day pack is sufficient. For loads of more than 10 pounds, you can get an expensive day pack with aluminum stays to fit the back's curves.

Small children carrying light loads don't need boots. Tennis shoes will do, so long as they fit well. Considering children's ability to get their feet wet, an extra pair of shoes is probably worth carrying, along with several extra pairs of socks. When your child begins to demand mountaineering boots like your own, a fair stopgap at one third the price is a pair of high work shoes from a retail clothing chain. These can be pretty well waterproofed (see Chapter 12). "Insulated" socks with a thick, spongy bottom avoid a lot of foot problems with children.

Clothing

Children's clothing should be in good condition when you start out, because it is going to get much hard use. For the same reason, try to avoid fashionable but flimsy garments. Be generous in the amount of warm clothing you bring for the child. The child who is usually a "heat machine" may get so exhausted that the machine is temporarily out of order.

Food and Cooking

It is even more important for the child than for the adult to snack often. Fill pockets in the children's packs with foods which they like and which provide quick energy, so they can snack

Children love to be around water

whenever they want. You should make good, nutritious food always available, while never urging your child to "eat something." Since you have simplified your menu, perhaps as far as one-pot meals, formal meals in camp will be the same for everyone. There is no room in the pack, or in the nutritional handbook, for those foods whose only attraction is their TV commercials.

Eating utensils for a child are the same as for anyone else. The oversize, heavy, interlocking knife-fork-and-spoon set is best reserved for car-camping. However, any child who will properly use and care for a small pocket knife should have one.

Planning Trips

Unless you are a leisurely, unambitious or infirm backpacker, a trip on which you take children should be shorter in days, shorter in miles, lower in elevation, and less steep in gradient than one you would plan for yourself. Decide on a trip that fits these requirements, then let the children in on the rest of the decisions. Let them help repackage the food. Have them make their own checklists of their own personal gear, and then have them pack it. Look over their packed packs. Make them justify anything in the pack that you think is unnecessary—but try to see their side of it.

Don't let the child carry too heavy a load. If they are under 10, they should carry less than one fourth of their body weight. If they are 10 or over, they can carry one fourth of their weight.

For the family that has never been on a backpack together, a "shakedown" weekend hike somewhere near home is very worthwhile. It will help you avoid bad things and multiply good things on the big trip.

If you feel you'd like to have a babysitter along, you can easily have one. Many young people are willing to go along and help out in return for free meals and the chance to spend some time in the wilds. An alternative to a babysitter is some other children for yours to play with. You may want to invite the other children's parents as companions for yourselves.

Trailhead Tips

When packing the luxuries that you will use while with your car, ask your children what things they want included. Along with your cold beer, pack their favorite thirst-quencher.

Children dawdle

Walking

When hiking with children, forget all my advice about a steady pace. They aren't buying it. Children want to dawdle, dally and delay. At least, those are the names an adult gives to what the child does. If the children are naming their activities at all, they think of them as pleasurable, and probably even necessary. *Their* negative words are reserved for any adult who enforces a schedule of so many miles by lunchtime, and so many more before dinner. Taking enough rest stops, then, is not a problem when kids are along.

Realizing this, you will try to keep yourself amused whenever your child stops to scrutinize a butterfly or climb onto a big log. And you will have alternative, nearer campsites in mind for the night.

The child who is too young to walk, or too young to walk all the way, must be carried. A kiddie carrier has some room for things besides the child—but someone else will have to carry a very large load.

Camping Techniques

When young children are along, the trip goes much better if you make camp by noon. In choosing a campsite, remember that water is very important to children. It doesn't seem to matter much what kind—lake, stream, pond or puddle—as long as there is some water for them to play in. The temperature of the water is not terribly important either. A snow bank near camp is another favorite play place.

If any of the children is only one or two years old, the camp should not be so close to water or to steep drop-offs that the little child can get into trouble. You must watch children that age like a hawk anyway. If they wander out of sight in the wilderness, they're lost. For this reason, a tent you can zip closed is desirable for the young one to sleep in.

Except for such a young one, let children pick their own bedsite—with gentle guidance if necessary. Have them set up their bed and then gather wood before they start to play. That is the rule for everyone arriving in camp.

Safety and Well-Being

On backpacking trips, children may become too tired, for any of several reasons. Being excited, they may not sleep well before the trip or on it. They are likely to be hyperactive. They don't sit still long enough to eat enough. To some extent, children will have to learn for themselves to slow down. You can help by being calm yourself, before and during the trip. In addition, don't get so immersed in your own activities that you fail to anticipate your children's needs. For instance, you know they will need sunburn protection and mosquito protection, whereas they wouldn't think of it by themselves until it was too late.

Children are especially vulnerable to sun and wind

Although children have a large amount of energy, and great powers of recuperation, remember that their bodies are much smaller and legs are much shorter than yours. A boulder you can step over is a major obstacle to five-year-olds, and they will expend much more energy than you will in getting across a field of boulders.

A preschool child may be upset by the lack of the accustomed home environment. You can prevent at least some of the upset by bringing along part of that home environment—a favorite toy, for instance.

In the first-aid kit, write children's dosages of pills on the labels. Young children have sensitive skins, so bring something to prevent chapping. *Desitin*, a diaper-rash ointment, is also good for hands and face.

If your child is a toddler, put a harness with "leash" on the child while the group is walking places that would be dangerous. Before you leave home, tell children what to do if lost. Review it with them until they understand it all. Every child should have a whistle on a string around their neck at all times and should understand they are to blow it only if lost—and then repeatedly. A child may wander too far simply because they got so engrossed following an animal's tracks or looking at the wildflowers that they forgot to look around now and then to make sure they could still locate the camp or the trail. They may not realize they're lost until they've been lost for a while. Be sure they know, therefore, that the *minute* they aren't sure they can find their way back, they should sit down in one spot and not move from it.

The greatest threat to children in the wilds is water. The number of drownings per year is staggering. Teach your children to respect the water—and even then, watch them like a hawk.

Map and Compass

Being inexhaustibly curious, children are ready at an early age to start learning about maps and compasses. As you walk along the trail with children, ask them every little while which way they think is north. If they're right, compliment them. If wrong, let them try again. At night, show them the North Star and explain how it's related to north on the compass and on the map. (Maybe you'll have to find out first.) As soon as your children can use a topographic map at all, give them their own to carry. Get them an inexpensive compass too.

Equipment Care

Until your children are well into their teens, you should check over their equipment with them and help them repair it if necessary.

daddy long legs and sonny short legs

14

• •

Recommended Reading

A great number of printed aids for backpacking are available free, and others are quite worth their modest price. From the federal government you can get several kinds of maps (see Chapter 11), summaries of the climate of particular regions, short how-to pamphlets on various aspects of backpacking, including how to administer first aid, and lists of campgrounds. For information, write the Superintendent of Documents, Washington, D.C. 20402.

Most backpacking-supply stores (see Appendix I) have catalogs, and many stores and equipment makers also give away little pamphlets on "How To Enjoy Backpacking" and the like.

Where To Go

The principal publisher of trail guides, emphasizing California, is **Wilderness Press, 2440 Bancroft Way, Berkeley, CA 94704**. Write for their catalog.

Other guide publishers:

The Appalachian Trial Conference
1718 N Street N.W.
Washington, D.C. 20036

The Appalachian Mountain Club
5 Joy St.
Boston, MA 02108

Falcon Press
P.O. Box 1718
Helena, MT 59624

Johnson Books
1880 South 57th Ct.
Boulder, CO 80301

The Mountaineers Books
1011 S.W. Klickitat Way. #107
Seattle, WA 98134

Pruett Publishing Co.
2928 Pearl St.
Boulder, CO 80301

How To Do It

The New Complete Walker III, by Colin Fletcher (New York: A. A. Knopf, 3rd ed., 1984), hard cover. This is the best book I know of about walking and backpacking. Unfortunately, it is not for novices: You have to know something about backpacking in order to profit from parts of the book.

Mountaineering: the Freedom of the Hills, edited by Don Graydon (Seattle: The Mountaineers, 5th ed., 1992), hard cover. This book is written for climbers, but the chapters on "Approaching the Peaks" contain much valuable advice from a number of people with vast experience.

Backpacking: One Step at a Time, by Harvey Manning (New York: Random House, 1986). Written with grace, humor and feeling by the Northwest's leading conservation editor-writer and hiker, this book distills the experiences of a large number of backpackers who work at the famous Seattle "Co-op," as well as the author's own experiences.

Basic Rockcraft, by Royal Robbins (Glendale, CA: La Siesta Press, rev. 1985). This book is included here for its information on using caribiners and slings, which are helpful in difficult stream crossings.

Simple Foods for the Pack, by Claudia Axcell et al. (San Francisco: Sierra, 2nd ed. 1986). For backpackers who prefer nonmeat meals with unprocessed foods, as well as those who would enjoy some delicious menu ideas, this book offers many tasty recipes.

Soft Paths: How to Enjoy Wilderness Without Harming It, by Bruce Hampton and David Cole (Harrisburg, PA: Stackpole Books, 1988). We could all use a little guidance on this subject.

Backpacking With Babies and Small Children, by Goldie Silverman (Berkeley: Wilderness Press: 2nd ed., 1986). A backpacking grandmother tells what she has learned about the subject over the many trips since she was a new mother in the wilderness. She also relays cogent suggestions from many other parents who have taken children into the wilds.

Desert Hiking, by Dave Ganci (Berkeley: Wilderness Press, 3rd ed., 1993). Hiking in the desert presents different problems from hiking in the mountains, and not just problems of water. This book presents some solutions.

Wilderness Cuisine, by Carole Latimer (Berkeley: Wilderness Press, 1991). This book tells how to have meals that are delicious as well as nutritious, even in the backcountry.

Widening Your Horizons

There are hundreds of field guides to birds, flowers, trees, animals, rocks, animal tracks, etc. In general, it is best to use one that was written for the region you are traveling in, rather than one that seeks to cover the whole country or the whole world.

Armchair adventure books written by hikers are also coming off the presses at a great rate. Some are fiction, some are fiction offered as fact, and some are quite authentic.

First Aid

Mountaineering Medicine, by Fred T. Darvill, Jr., M.D. (Berkeley: Wilderness Press, 13th ed., 1992) focuses on backpacking and mountaineering specifically.

The American Red Cross First Aid and Safety Handbook, by the American Red Cross Staff. (New York: Little, Brown, 1992). The Red Cross is the most authoritative body for first-aid advice.

Appendix I

Mail-Order Companies with Backpacking Equipment

California

Alpenlite
3891 N. Ventura
Ventura, CA 93001

Garcia Machine (bear-
  resistant containers)
14097 Ave. 272
Visalia, CA 93292
(209) 732-3785

Marmot Mountain Works
3049 Adeline St.
Berkeley, CA 94703
(800) MARMOT9

Moonstone Mountaineering
1563 G St.
Arcata, CA 95521
(707) 826-0851

Wilderness Experience
2072 Dearborn St.
Chatsworth, CA 91311
(818) 341-5774

Colorado

Frostline Kits
252 River Rd.
Grand Junction, CO 81505
(303) 241-0156

Maine

L.L. Bean
Freeport, ME 04033
(800) 221-4221

Moss Tents
P.O. Box 309
Camden, ME 04843
(207) 236-8368

New Hampshire

Stephenson Warmlite
22 Hook Rd.
Gilford, NH 03246
(603) 293-8526

New Jersey

Campmor
810 Route 17 N.
Paramus, N.J. 07653
(201) 445-5000

Washington

Mountain Safety Research
4225 Second Ave. S.
Seattle, WA 98134
(206) 624-8573

Recreational Equipment, Inc.
Sumner, WA 98352-0001
(800) 426-4840

Swallow's Nest
2308 Sixth Ave.
Seattle, WA 98121
(800) 676-4041

Mail-Order Lightweight-Food Stores

AlpineAire
P.O. Box 926
Nevada City, CA 95959
(800) 322-6325

Perma-Pak
230 E. 6400 S.
Murray, UT 84107
(801) 268-9915

Recreational Equipment, Inc.
Sumner, WA 98352-0001
(800) 426-4840

Stow-A-Way Products
P.O. Box 957
East Greenwich, RI 02818
(401) 885-6899

Wee Pak
P.O. Box 562
Sun Valley, ID 83353
(800) 722-2710

Appendix II

Checklist for Packing

The only way to avoid forgetting things is to make and use a checklist. Not every trip will require the same things. It depends on who's going, how long you will be in the wilderness, what time of year it is, and other things. Your checklist should include everything you might want. Simply ignore the things that are not appropriate for your present trip. Until you develop your own checklist, use the one below. Regarding each item, ask yourself, "Can I do without it?" Be ruthless.

To wear or carry in a readily accessible place

hat or cap
dark glasses
shirt
pants
belt
boots
socks
sunscreen
bandana
underwear
maps
compass
waterproof matches
toilet paper
watch
knife

insect repellent
lip balm
first-aid kit
rain garment
flashlight
whistle
pencil and paper (for leaving
  notes)
drinking cup
water bottle
fishing license
wilderness permit
camera and film
one quarter
quick-energy food
water purifier

To carry in the pack

tent or tarp
sleeping bag
ground sheet

braided nylon cord
collapsible plastic bucket
plastic bags—assorted

air mattress or pad
pillowcase
extra shirt
extra pants
extra underwear
extra socks
jacket, sweater or vest
camp shoes or moccasins
gloves
knit cap or balaclava
extra bandanas
duct tape
sewing kit
*extra prescription glasses
extra flashlight batteries
    and bulb

rubber bands
candle
towel
food
cooking gear
*grate
plastic bowl
spoon
*fishing tackle
*book
*camera equipment
*musical instrument
*binoculars
toothbrush
toothpaste or powder
comb or brush

*optional

To do before you leave home (depending)

write for fire permit
write for wilderness permit
get latest road maps
stop newspaper delivery
give itinerary to friend, with phone number of area administrators
arrange for someone to take in your mail
check money and credit-card supplies
take one last look around house for what you forget to pack

Appendix III

Conservation organizations

The price of wilderness, like the price of liberty, is eternal vigilance. Someone is always about to carve off a piece of wilderness to use for tree cutting, mining, ski resorts or something else. If you always want to have nice places to go backpacking, you'll have to expend a little effort to help save these places. Fortunately, there are a number of existing organizations that are already set up to work for wilderness. They simply need your help.

I urge you to get in touch with any or all of the organizations listed below, and join the ones that seem best to you.

Appalachian Mountain Club
5 Joy St.
Boston, MA 02108

American Hiking Society
P.O. Box 20160
Washington, D.C. 20041

California Wilderness
  Coalition
2655 Portage Bay East
Davis, CA 95616

The Mountaineers
300 Third Ave., W.
Seattle, WA 98119

National Parks and
  Conservation Association
1776 Massachusetts Ave.
  N.W.
Washington, D.C. 20036

Sierra Club
730 Polk St.
San Francisco, CA 94109

The Wilderness Society
900 17th St. N.W.
Washington, D.C. 20006-
  2596

The Author's Pack

On the next page is a photograph of the contents of my pack, alongside a key to identify each thing. In the photograph is everything needed for two people for two nights and two days, except my companion's personal things.

(On the other hand, the picture does not show the "tools of the trade" that I carry to gather information and data for the trail guides I write: a tape recorder, a second camera, a telephoto lens, a thermometer, several maps, and several field guides to flora and fauna.)

Contents of author's pack

(everything for 2 people for 2 nights except second person's individual gear)

1. Sun hat
2. Gore-Tex rain parka
3. Wool hat
4. Gloves
5. Pile jacket
6. Polypro long underwear bottoms
7. Long-sleeved shirt
8. Underwear
9. Bandana
10. Long pants
11. Extra wool socks
12. Extra liner socks
13. Toothbrush
14. Toilet paper
15. Personal items in zippered pouch
16. Mosquito repellent
17. Mosquito-proof head net
18. Sunblock
19. Breakfast food
20. Lunch food
21. Dinner food
22. Towel
23. First-aid kit
24. Nalgene 1-quart water bottle
25. Binoculars
26. Eating bowl
27. Drinking cup
28. Camera
29. Salt and pepper
30. Sunglasses
31. Zippered pouch containing: repair kit (consisting of a couple of feet of duct tape wrapped around an aluminum sleeve), matches in waterproof container, Lexan spoon, lighter, Lexan fork, Swiss Army knife
32. Topographic map
33. Compass
34. Dish rag
35. Flashlight
36. Tent
37. Pack
38. Water filter
39. Sleeping pad
40. Sleeping bag
41. Nesting cooking pots
42. Pot scrubber
43. Stove
44. Fuel bottle
45. Nylon line
46. Camp shoes
47. Rain cover for pack

Index

author's pack 131–33
bandana 37
bear bagging 79–85
bears 56, 79, 85
blisters 7, 98
books 66, 121–24
boots 5–7, 66, 98, 107, 108, 112
breathability of fabrics 16, 35
campfire 48, 50, 85–87
campsite 73–80, 116
checklist 5, 59, 60, 127–28
children, taking 111–19
companions 55, 97
compass 97, 102–06, 118
conditioning 57, 68
conservation organizations 129
cord 28, 80–83
Cryptosporidium 26
dehydrated food 39, 40, 42–43, 46
dehydration 47
dishwashing 52
down, goose 15, 16
duct tape 107
Ensolite 17
fireplace 73, 74, 78, 85–87
first aid 89
first-aid kit 89–90, 97, 118
flashlight 24–25
food 39–46, 51, 60, 78, 79, 114
freeze-dried food 39, 40–41, 43–44
garbage 89
Giardia 26
gloves 38
Gore-Tex 16, 22, 31, 32, 35, 108
hat 36–37, 87
hypothermia 94–96, 98
knife 25, 87, 97, 109
lantern 65
layering of clothes 29–33
lightning 94
lost, being 97
mail-order companies 125–26
maps 97
map wheel 104
mattress 15, 17–18, 63, 79
minimum impact 50, 78, 85–87, 88–89

mosquitoes 99, 117
mountain sickness 92
pack 5, 7–13, 60–62, 109, 112, 114
pants 35
paper towels 27
parka 32–33
pets 55–56
pillow 17, 19
poison ivy 93
poison oak 93
polypropylene 30
poncho 35–37
rain pants 33
river crossings 99–102
shirt 35
Sierra Club 55
sleeping bag 5, 13–17, 29, 31, 60,
   77, 87–88, 94, 96 107–08, 112
socks 6–7, 87, 98
solo 55
Stephenson, Jack 34
stove 48–50, 53, 65
sunburn 92–93, 117
sweat, insensible 33
sweat, sensible 33
swimsuit 37, 66
tarp 19–22, 179
tent 5, 19–22, 53, 61, 79, 88, 109–10
Therm-a-Rest 18
ticks 93
toilet 88
toilet paper 27, 88
topographic maps 103–06
tube tent 22, 79
underwear 30
vapor barriers 33–35
water bottle 27, 47
water bucket 47
water purifying 26
Whisperlite stove 49
wilderness permits 102
wilderness preservation 59
wind 75–76, 79, 93
wood 48, 86–87
zipper repair 109–10